"Sexy, funny, heartbreaking, terrifying.... I hear Robert Rosen singing a universal song, and I love it!" —Thomas E. Kennedy, author of *In the Company of Angels*

Bobby in Naziland

A TALE OF FLATBUSH

BY ROBERT ROSEN

"A compelling portrait of a time and a place that no longer exists.... Rosen's book is speaking for a generation."
—*The Huffington Post*

HEADPRESS

"A poignant sketch of Flatbush during a time when the borough lost the Dodgers and the nation lost its innocence. Compulsively readable, especially for Boomers." —Doug Garr, former speechwriter for New York governor Mario Cuomo; author of *Between Heaven and Earth: An Adventure in Free Fall*

"This is history writ with piss and vinegar, stark, unsentimental, and unexpectedly moving.... A repository of postwar Jewish memory of the sort that historians can't find in archives." —Whitney Strub, history professor and director of Women's and Gender Studies, Rutgers University–Newark; author of *Perversion for Profit: The Politics of Pornography and the Rise of the New Right*

"You might call this remarkable coming-of-age memoir a kosher *Catcher in the Rye*, if it weren't in a category all its own.... Brilliant, darkly comic... its characters are unforgettable and deeply moving." —David Comfort, author of *The Rock and Roll Book of the Dead* and *An Insider's Guide to Publishing*; contributor to Blogcritics.org

"Truth seeps out of every paragraph.... Wry, touching, and disturbingly insightful." —B. A. Nilsson, arts critic for *Words and Music*

"Bold and beautiful! Hilarious and deeply meaningful.... Poignant and sensuous." —A. D. Hitchin, author of *Prince: Purple Reign*; co-editor of the *CUT UP!* anthology

"Compassionate, well told and sensitive." —Darius H. James, author of *Negrophobia*

"This reads as if Anne Frank had a younger, surviving brother who continued her diaries.... You feel the same honest, innocent, and candid perception of the world from a child's point of view." —J. C. Malone, syndicated columnist for *Listin Diario* (Dominican Republic)

For Brooklyn

Table of Contents

"I was a schmuck, too. I lived in Brooklyn."

"I remained poor and depressed, as
 a Brooklyn child should."

—Maurice Sendak
The New Yorker, May 21, 2012

1

The *Goyim* and the Jews

First of all, I didn't call them *goyim*. My parents and grandparents called them goyim. I knew what the word meant; I knew hundreds of Yiddish words, maybe a thousand. I just never used them because they sounded too... Jewish. Yiddish was the language old Jews spoke when they didn't want young Jews to understand what they were saying. So I didn't call the goyim anything, even though our building was full of them.

Mostly they were Catholics, like the Coogans, who lived on the ground floor. At first there were five Coogans: James Sr., Mary, Stephanie, James Jr., and Christopher. Then when I was five, Gary was born, and soon after that, Mary, whom my mother called "the *shikse*," was pregnant again. It began to seem as if she were popping out a new kid as often as their dog, Queenie, was popping out a litter, which was just about every year.

"Why does Mary have so many babies?" I asked my mother, who had only me.

"Because they're Catholic," she said, which, as far as she was concerned, explained everything I needed to know about Catholics in general and the Coogans in particular—like why

Bobby in Naziland

they hung over every bed in their apartment a bloody, agonized Jesus on a cross that horrified me every time I went to visit them and eat their goyim food slathered in goyim condiments; or why James Jr., Stephanie, and Christopher went to Holy Innocents, rather than PS 249, where they learned that the Jews killed Christ (though they didn't seem to hold me personally responsible); or why Mary washed out James Jr.'s and Christopher's mouths with soap every time they took the Lord's name in vain. This was a punishment my mother held over my own head like the Sword of Damocles, should she ever hear a "dirty word" spout from my lips. But she never inflicted this cruelty upon me, not because she never heard me say "fuck" or "shit," and not even after our next-door neighbor Mrs. McAllister told her that I was standing in front of the house shouting "*Fuck!*" at the top of my lungs. She never did it because that was physical child abuse, and enlightened Jews trafficked only in the emotional kind.

And she never stopped me from hanging around with the Coogans, or any other goyim, for that matter, even though she preferred I spend my time in the company of Jews—except for Jeffrey Abromovitz, who lived in the building next door. My mother must have known that Abromovitz, though he possessed only a vague awareness of what a vagina was, had taken it upon himself to teach me everything he knew about sex, usually as we walked to and from Hebrew school, though occasionally he'd instruct me in the privacy of my bedroom, telling me that "fucking is when you put your dick in a girl's ass" and that "babies come out of the cunt," which he said was "the size of a pinhole" before asking me, "Do you know what *rape* means?"

I'd heard the word but didn't know what it meant, so I took my best guess: "It's when you strip a girl."

"No," he said, "it's when you put your dick in a girl's ass

2

when she doesn't want you to."

"It is not," I objected, having a hard time getting my mind around the idea that sometimes a girl *did* want you to put your dick in her ass.

Or maybe my mother found out that Abromovitz, who knew that I coveted his ultra-rare Roger Maris baseball card, #1 in the Topps series that year, had agreed to give it to me if I'd lick the sidewalk in front of his house 61 times, once for each home run Maris hit in '61. Which I did—and then felt so angry and humiliated, I took my new Maris card home, stashed it in a safe place, pried open a dead dry-cell battery and, unaware that the black gunk inside was battery acid, went back outside and smeared it on the head of Abromovitz's best friend, Michael Mendel, because Abromovitz was always giving him baseball cards for free, even if he didn't have a double.

I thought Mendel might try to punch me, but instead he burst into tears and ran home, and Abromovitz ran home, too, to tell his mother what I'd done—which naturally led to my permanent banishment from the Abromovitz household, not to mention the beginnings of a reputation among certain neighborhood parents as a bad influence, a wild and malicious kid, and a troublemaker capable of wanton violence.

Which was true, though I was hardly the worst that Flatbush had to offer. Not even close. For one thing, I'd never been arrested, so I wasn't, technically, a "juvenile delinquent." In fact, I was an angel compared to the shoemaker's son, Frankie Pizzello, who everybody knew had been going around breaking kneecaps for the Mob since he was 14, or Aileen Murphy, who prowled Church Avenue with a vicious black mutt she called "Nigger," and who, according to what I'd heard people say on street corners, had once been sent away to reform school—at age 11, for the crime

Bobby in Naziland

of being a "*hooah*"—where, it was widely believed, "they sewed up her cunt to stop her from fucking."

Other people pulsed with energy far more violent than my own, and they aren't the kind of people you could forget, even if you wanted to. I would, for example, like to forget Alan Feldman, one of the Jews who lived in my building. Though he was only a year older than I was, he outweighed me by a good hundred pounds, and though he beat me up only once, flinging me to the ground and then sitting on me, it was an all-too-memorable beating, administered in front of a half-dozen of his jeering friends—one of whom I'd never forgiven for destroying the igloo I'd built in front of the house the previous winter—just to teach me to shut the fuck up and maybe think twice before I ever again told him to his face, incorrectly, "You're too fat to take me."

And I didn't care for Feldman's fat father, either. Because Mr. Feldman, a bus driver—a "professional driver," as his son called him—was a dead ringer for that other bus driver, Ralph Kramden, the unfunniest sitcom character on TV. The sight of Mr. Feldman, in full Transit Authority regalia, perched on the windowsill of his first-floor apartment, watching with pride as his son stomped on the head of some unfortunate soul who'd happened to wander by at the wrong time, made *The Honeymooners* look to me like cinéma vérité.

My downstairs neighbor Brian Riley, who lived next door to the Coogans, comes to mind, too—though for entirely different reasons. The first time I ever set foot in a bar was when Brian took me with him to the Maple Court Tavern, on Church Avenue, to provide moral support as he hit up his stepfather, Patrick, for money. Patrick, who whiled away most afternoons knocking back whiskey shots and highballs at this "gin mill" (as my father called every dive on Church Avenue), made a big show of giving

4

Brian 50 cents. He then invited us to join him at the bar for a round of 7-Ups, but I declined because I thought my parents would kill me if they ever found out I was drinking in bars with the goyim (whom I didn't call goyim).

But the main reason I remember that afternoon is because of what happened about two hours later, when Patrick came stumbling home from the Maple Court as Brian and I were playing Chinese handball in front of the house with the Spaldeen he'd just bought in my father's candy store.

"I thought I told you not to wear white socks with black shoes," Patrick said to Brian, and then smacked him across the face with the back of his hand.

Brian just stood there, expressionless.

"You better watch out or you're getting the strap tonight," Patrick said before walking into the building.

"That's what the goyim do," my mother explained when I told her what had happened. "They drink, and then they come home and beat their kids. Aren't you glad we're not like that?"

My mother was always telling me that I should be glad that she wasn't like a lot of our neighbors—Celine, for example, the morbidly obese hairstylist who lived in Abromovitz's building, and who, in 1958, began dying her hair in a rainbow of colors, one after another, like bright purple, cobalt blue, and, on occasion, shocking pink. Everybody on East 17th Street would stop whatever they were doing to watch, mesmerized, as this woman, whom I knew little about beyond what I saw—I didn't even know her last name—emerged from her first-floor apartment and waddled towards the fire-engine-red van that was parked in front of her house. Poised behind the wheel of this customized "Fatmobile" (as most people called it)—it had special doors and seats to accommodate her—was her Jack Sprat husband, waiting to chauffeur her to the beauty parlor where she worked. And as the van pulled away, we'd all look at each other, mouths agape, shaking our heads, as if we'd witnessed a natural phenomenon so rare and spectacular, it left us without means of expression.

There were a number of noteworthy people, too, over on the next block, East 18th Street. Lisa Horowitz, who lived in the building directly across the alleyway from my bedroom window, I'll always remember because of two incidents. The first was that afternoon in the second grade when, as our mothers talked Mahjong in the kitchen, she allowed me to wrestle her to my bedroom floor, pull up her plaid skirt, pull down her black tights, and caress her ass, as soft and smooth and white as anything I'd ever touched.

Then, looking me in the eye as she squirmed beneath my hand, she said, "Is that what you wanted to do?"

"Yes," I told her, amazed that she let me keep doing it for a long time, though after that she never let me do it again, despite my persistent efforts to persuade her otherwise: "Oh, come on... *please*... just for a second."

The other incident occurred that summer, when Lisa's mother, Anita, invited me and my mother to spend a few days in the bungalow they'd rented for two weeks near a lake upstate, in Dutchess County. Not only was driving up to the country absolutely thrilling, as this would be the farthest from home I'd ever been, but, when we got there, the only place for me to sleep, Anita and my mother agreed, was in a double bed with Lisa.

I don't know why they thought this was a good idea, though I suppose it's possible that my mother, unaware of the ass-feeling episode, had reason to doubt my heterosexual inclinations. Perhaps she'd sensed that I'd taken to exploring the contours of sexuality with one of my classmates, Arthur Blumenkrantz, who liked to grab my dick (as well as the dicks of a number of other classmates) when I had a "boner," as he called it. Once, we were sitting on the floor of my room, after school, playing chess, and we both had boners, there was no hiding it. So we took them out to compare, touching them head to head to see how it felt—electrifying. And it was at that moment that my mother pounded on the bedroom door and then, a second later, barged in, though she saw nothing but two guilt-ridden faces.

So there I was that night in the country, alone in a big double bed with Lisa, both of us in our pajamas. The only problem was that soon after our arrival that morning, I'd come down with a stomach virus, "a 24-hour bug," my mother called it. And the nausea that I felt came in horrible waves that obliterated both my little erection and my desire to touch Lisa's warm body, so close to me and so available, resulting in a night that passed in total innocence and occasional bouts of vomiting.

David Nachmann, the "neighborhood genius," lived upstairs from Lisa, and my mother was always holding him up as a shining example of everything I should be but wasn't: ambitious, obedient, and possessed of a nose-to-the-grindstone work ethic.

"Why can't you get the kind of marks David Nachmann does? You have the same I.Q.," she'd tell me every time I brought home a less than stellar "underachiever's" report card, which was pretty much every time. "He's going to get into Harvard. You keep it up and you'll be lucky if you get into a community college."

Most of us in our so-called "intellectually gifted" class thought that Nachmann's father, an electronics engineer, was the one who built the computers that Nachmann turned in for his science projects in the first and second grades—his second-grade computer a quantum leap in sophistication over the one he'd submitted the previous year. Then, in the third grade, his father, aged 35, dropped dead from a heart attack. So what did Nachmann do? He brought to school a *supercomputer* full of dials and lights and switches, the likes of which we'd never seen before. And nobody, not even our teacher, Mrs. Feinstein, understood how this contraption was able to do all manner of mathematical calculations, including square roots, which we hadn't even learned about yet. So Nachmann won the science fair again, hands-down, and though everybody was whispering it to each other, not one of us dared say to Nachmann's face that his father must have built the computer before he died.

Eugene Appelberg, Nachmann's upstairs neighbor, was his chief rival for the title of smartest, most ambitious kid in the class, and he'd been on TV, too—on *Wonderama*, the Sunday morning kids' show on channel five. The host, Sonny Fox, had picked him out of the audience and asked him what he wanted to be when he grew up ("A lawyer," he said, "so I can sue people"), where he lived, and where he went to school. I was flabbergasted. I'd never seen anybody I knew on TV before. But that's not why I remember him. Rather, it's because at a time when "normal" people ate meat every day and all it took to be branded a "weirdo" was to bring a container of yogurt to school for a recess snack, Appelberg and his mother, whom my mother called "Chiquita"—she said she dressed like the cartoon character in the Chiquita Banana commercial—were vegetarians, which was as scandalous as being a Communist, if not more so. And there was no father in the picture, which added to the weirdness. All this, of course, made Appleberg the target of unrelenting and merciless ridicule, and as if that weren't enough to permanently embed him in our collective memories, in the fifth grade, a space heater set his pajamas on fire and he nearly burned to death. So how did we greet Eugene the morning he returned to school after spending nearly a year in the hospital, getting skin grafts and whatnot? With two-dozen variations on, "Hey, Appelberg, got any bananas? I saw your mother sellin' 'em on TV!" Then we took turns goosing him and grabbing his dick.

As for what's become of these random people I've plucked from the annals of my memory, I've no idea. I can't find any of them on the Internet, not even Nachmann, who you'd think would have founded a company like Microsoft by now. My old neighbors seem to exist only in my head—though some of them must be out there somewhere, perhaps wondering what's become of me, that kid they used to see either hanging around the candy store or slugging it out in the street, for no discernable reason, with half the other kids in the neighborhood.

But I did have my reasons, discernable or otherwise. Take that fight I picked with Alan Feldman. I did it because, in addition to his fat face and his fat father the bus driver, I didn't like his vibe, not that I called it a vibe, but that's what it was. And that's why I punched out at least one of the three Alesio brothers every week, even though they spent a fortune in the candy store on baseball cards and wooden gliders. I don't know why the sight of them made me crazy. It just did. Or maybe it was because the whole neighborhood, including me, was suffering from an epidemic of what was not yet called post-traumatic stress disorder.

That's probably why the sight of the husky kid with the crew cut—the one who walked by my house every day on his way home from school—made me crazy, too. All I knew about him was that he was Catholic, because like all the Catholic kids he went to Holy Innocents and wore their stupid uniform, the gray blazer and the blue tie with the "HI" monogram.

Bobby in Naziland

One afternoon as he walked by, he purposely bumped into me. So I belted him in his mouth, and everybody who was hanging out in front of the building gathered around us in a circle to scream for blood. And boy, did we ever try to give it to them. Spurred on by the cheering and jeering, we threw wild, roundhouse punches, doing all we could to knock each other out cold with a good shot to the jaw, like we saw on TV. But even when we connected, the best we could do was send each other staggering backwards in a fog, before we came at each other again, fists flailing and murder in our eyes. And no matter how hard we pounded each other's faces, we just couldn't score that knockout—because we were kids, for Christ's sake, ignorant mini-punks who lacked the common sense to walk away from a fight and lacked the punching power to do any real damage (though I often did come home with torn pants, which drove my mother nuts).

That was life on East 17th Street—a street I'd lived on for so long, I couldn't imagine *not* living on it; a street on which I got to know, in an intimate, visceral way, not just the people I fought with every day, but every tangible thing that made up the block: the alleyways, the buildings, their cellars—some of them converted into fallout shelters and stocked with giant khaki-colored cans filled with soda crackers and Kotex. With the building I lived in (and played Chinese handball in front of), I knew every crack in the sidewalk cement, I knew every brick that comprised the street-level masonry, I knew the mortar in between the bricks, and I knew especially well those two Doric columns in front, which it was my joy to climb upon, to cling to, and to press my cheek against and feel the coolness of the fluted gray stone.

From the day we moved to East 17th Street, when I was one, until the day, 12 years later, that we moved away, I never left the street for more than two weeks, and for 11 of those 12 years, only once did I travel more than a hundred miles away: In the fifth grade, my parents took me to Washington, D.C., a family vacation that seemed so miraculous and exotic that when we drove across the border from New Jersey into Delaware, a state I'd never been to before, I demanded that my father pull the car over so I could get out and walk around, as if we'd just landed on the moon.

East 17th was like a street frozen in amber—a place where time stood still. Yes, an abandoned house had burned to the ground one night in 1957, and in its place a luxury apartment building popped up. And yes, babies were occasionally born, especially to the Catholic families. But people rarely moved away, and they didn't seem to die very often, either, at least the ones I knew, which meant that new people rarely moved in.

I was so sick of East 17th Street, the moment my parents allowed me to wander beyond its confines, I set out for the far reaches of Flatbush (or *Flapbush*, as native Flatbushians pronounced it), eager to inspect all the landmarks I'd been looking at through car windows but had never had the opportunity to explore. A prominent one was the Dutch Reformed Church, on Flatbush Avenue, a square block where time really had stood still for 200 years. I'd wander through its ancient graveyard, reading the fading inscriptions on the weathered tombstones, often of kids my own age, whose bones now lay beneath my feet, and I'd try to imagine what they were like when they were alive and living in Flatbush, in 1754, when it was all farmland. Then I'd walk across the street and gaze in awe and intimidation at the looming Gothic edifice of the oldest high school in America, Erasmus, where *Jewish* Barbra Streisand and *Jewish* Bobby Fischer, the weirdest of the weirdos, had once hung out together and stridden its

Bobby in Naziland

hallowed halls, anonymous and hungry for immortality. Or if I had 50 cents on me, I might go see a good horror film, like *House of Usher*—Edgar Allan Poe's premature-burial story, which was so good I had trouble sleeping for months after I saw it—at one of the rococo, multi-tiered Flatbush Avenue movie palaces, like the Albemarle, the Astor, the Rialto, or the Loew's (pronounced *Lowie's*) Kings.

It was at the Kings, one afternoon in 1962, after sitting through a showing of *The Three Stooges in Orbit*, that I saw the *Jewish* Stooges themselves run down the aisles and take to the stage as every kid in the packed house simultaneously let loose with an ear-shattering shriek. And yes, Larry's hair *was* real, we saw it up close, thus settling that debate. (Also, it was true, as we found out later, that Moe Howard, aka Moses Horwitz, had gone to Erasmus—in 1915—but, seduced by the siren call of showbiz, dropped out after a couple of months to make his way in the wider world beyond *Flapbush*.)

Once I was allowed to cross Caton Avenue on my own, I could play baseball anytime I wanted, though not terribly well, on the sacred, scruffy sandlots of the Parade Grounds, where, before he was crowned King of the Jews because he refused to pitch a World Series game on Yom Kippur, Sandy Koufax, on the road to the Hall of Fame, had learned to throw his unhittable curve ball. And I played tackle football there, too, without protective gear, a game I *was* good at because I could run fast, I liked to hit, and I didn't drop the ball. These were the only skills you needed to excel at this chaotic sport, which was little more than an organized street brawl—though I also studied the offensive and defensive diagrams I found in magazines and applied them as best I could to what I did on the playing field. Sometimes on Saturday afternoons, when he wasn't working in the candy store, my father came to watch me play. He'd stand quietly on the sidelines and then tell me after the game, "You've got guts, kid, but you don't know what you're doing."

A block from my house in the other direction stood two red brick monoliths inscribed with "CHVRCH AVENVE," the "U"s rendered as "V"s, as was done in ancient Rome. They marked the frontier of another world, Prospect Park South. This mini-neighborhood's eerily serene, gracefully curving, seemingly depopulated boulevards were shaded by a canopy of old-growth maples and lined with sprawling, eccentric mansions whose inhabitants I so rarely saw, I sometimes wondered if they existed at all. One house, on Buckingham Road, looked like a Chinese pagoda. Another, on Albemarle Road, looked like a plantation house from *Gone with the Wind*, a veritable Tara with an attached greenhouse that could have accommodated my entire apartment with room to spare. A third house, on Rugby Road, was a weird gingerbread castle, originally built in England, then taken apart stone by stone and reassembled here. I'd walk these streets in a semi-dream state, looking at the magnificent abodes as if my nose were pressed to a pane of glass, barely able to imagine living in one and knowing I never would.

Yes, these diverse vistas offered tantalizing hints of paradise around every corner, but to me Flatbush felt more like a prison than a Garden of Eden. And like any prisoner, I was bored out of my mind only slightly more often than I was terrified by the simmering undercurrent of potential violence, both the kind generated daily by my East 17th Street neighbors and the kind perpetrated by the "bloodthirsty hoodlums" my parents and classmates were always talking about: marauding packs of Negroes (as the more enlightened among us called them) and Puerto Ricans from adjacent neighborhoods and boroughs, who, we'd heard, would use knives and do significant bodily harm when stealing our bicycles, lunch money, and anything else we had that was worth stealing. We'd even heard that sometimes they just murdered people for no reason, like "The Capeman," Salvador Agron, a Puerto Rican teenager and leader of the Vampires street gang, had done in a Manhattan playground. Wearing a red-lined black satin cape, Agron had stabbed to death, with a silver dagger (as the tabloids always noted), two Irish kids he'd mistaken for rival gang members—thereby cementing among "right-thinking" Flatbushians the vicious reputation of all Puerto Rican teenagers.

I'd neglected to give this perspective its proper due when my uncle Paul, my mother's younger brother, gave me a fishing pole and well-stocked tackle box for my ninth birthday. Though previously forbidden from going to notoriously crime-ridden Prospect Park without adult supervision, I was so eager to try out my new fishing gear, my mother allowed me to go "just this once"—with my friend Barry Gardner for protection, whatever that was worth.

The park looked disarmingly beautiful on this steamy August Saturday, its unkempt greenery overhanging the cesspool we called a lake, on which dozens of people were paddling around in rented rowboats and from which I'd seen my uncle pull out a multitude of sunfish and exactly one bass.

Barry and I went to my uncle's favorite fishing spot, a little peninsula behind the Greek Temple.

The quintet of Puerto Rican teenagers appeared out of nowhere as I was attaching a float and a lure to the line, positioning themselves in a semicircle and trapping us on the narrow spit of land. As soon as I saw them I understood what I was confronting: the barbaric, brown-skinned "other" from beyond the protective wall of psychic energy that surrounded most parts of Flatbush, the malevolent representatives of the murderous Capeman's tribe that I'd been warned about so many times. And even in my naïveté I understood what they saw: easy prey, a couple of "rich" white kids, half their size, one of whom had brand-new fishing gear.

Barry, frozen to the spot, looked at me and I could see the terror in his eyes. I think he expected to die. I turned around to look out on the lake for help, but nobody in the rowboats was paying any attention to us.

The oldest one in the group looked to be about 16, The Capeman's age at the time he committed the murders. He was tall and lanky, as I imagined The Capeman to be.

"Let me borrow your fishing pole," he said in perfect English, his tone friendly, his friends watching with detached curiosity.

"No," I told him, holding on to the rod and tackle box as tightly as I could.

He took a step closer and grabbed the rod, his hand partially covering mine, and in a business-like manner said, "Let go or I'll break your fingers."

"No, it's mine!"

"He'll do it," Barry whispered. "Give it to him."

I knew he was right, and I loosened my grip. The teenager yanked the rod and tackle box from my hands and walked off calmly, his four friends trailing behind him. They vanished into the park like smoke.

I was stunned. It had all happened so fast.

"My mother's going to kill me," I said, and began to cry.

Instead, she just banned me from ever again, under any circumstances, setting foot in Prospect Park without adult supervision—a ban that would last about two years, which is the equivalent of a liftime when you're nine.

As frightening as that robbery might have been, it was still the exception, and the more immediate threat to my personal safety was the perpetual proximity of the older, stronger kids on my block, like Alan Feldman and his gang of gargoyles, who I feared might decide at any given moment to kick my ass up and down East 17th Street for the sheer pleasure of it. That didn't happen very often, either, but how many times do you have to get your ass kicked for it to instill a righteous fear? One time will indeed do the trick, and I walked around most days filled with righteous fear, not just of Puerto Rican gangs and Fat Feldman and his friends, but also of random street toughs spoiling for a fight. One day two kids, probably a year older than I was, started following me around, intimating that they were going to beat me to a pulp. I didn't know who they were or why they wanted to beat me up—not that they needed a reason—and as one of them approached, apparently to begin dispensing this savage beating, I grabbed his head and smashed it repeatedly as hard as I could against a lamppost, until blood started oozing from his mouth and nose. Then I ran away as fast as I could while his friend shouted, "We're gonna *kill* you the next time we see you!"

I had no doubt, and a year must have passed before I realized there would be no next time.

From the upper floors of certain apartment buildings I could see the gleaming towers of Manhattan across the East River, 20 minutes and 15 cents away by subway, or a free trip if you were small enough to walk under the turnstile, which my mother encouraged me to do long after I was actually small enough... anything to save 15 cents. She practically dared token-booth clerks to say something, but they never did.

I enjoyed the game, too, and developed a fluid fare-beating technique, part Groucho-crouch, part duck-walk, part limbo. I did it so fast, the clerks rarely noticed, and it gave me an adrenaline rush every time, though other people, like my friends' parents, found it embarrassing when they took me with them on the subway and I slipped under the turnstile before they could drop in a token.

"Don't do that!" they'd cry.

"Why not? My mother lets me do it."

My mother and I made the trip to Manhattan about once a month, usually on a Saturday afternoon, catching the Brighton Express at Church Avenue, the station next door to the candy store. We'd push our way into the subway car, rushing to grab one of the padded wicker seats or positioning ourselves so I could hold on to one of the smooth enameled poles because I couldn't reach the handles hanging from the top of the car. Then I'd take it all in: the slowly spinning ceiling fans, like you'd see in a tropical café; the bare incandescent light bulbs; the "Miss Subways" posters and cigarette ads; the faces of my fellow straphangers, a mosaic of blankness.

The train would lurch forward and I'd gaze out the grimy windows as we passed Parkside Avenue and then stopped at the last open-air station, Prospect Park, where Ebbets Field used to be, before plunging into the blackness of the tunnel to make our way towards the Manhattan Bridge for the journey across the East River, gray and churning hundreds of feet below. This was the best part of the trip, the breathtaking vista of the Manhattan skyline coming ever closer, as Brooklyn—looking like a diminutive mountain range of church steeples and one lone Everest of a skyscraper, the Williamsburgh Savings Bank Building, where my dentist was—faded into the distance until we again plunged into the darkness beneath Manhattan.

These forays into "the city," as every Brooklynite called it, were invariably "educational," our destination often the 81st Street stop on Central Park West for the Museum of Natural History. My mother took me there because I liked to see the great blue whale suspended from the ceiling, and the reconstructed dinosaur skeletons, most of which I could identify by sight: brontosaurus, stegosaurus, triceratops, tyrannosaurus, allosaurus, pterodactyl... they had them all, along with their eggs and footprints. But afterwards, we never went into the famous park across the street, even in broad daylight, because it was "too dangerous." And we never lingered in the city to eat at a restaurant because, my mother said, "I can cook a better meal at home for a lot less money." We never went to a Broadway show, either, because it was too expensive, and we never went downtown to wander on the crazy crisscrossing cobblestone streets of Greenwich Village, though I don't know why, as this was free. And we certainly never visited anybody in Manhattan because we didn't know anybody who lived there, though I'd overheard my mother talking to my father about a distant and wealthy cousin—a doctor!—who lived on Central Park South but had never invited us to his house.

Manhattan might as well have been Oz, a place meant only for brief visitations, a place I didn't belong—because real people didn't live in Manhattan; it was as expensive as living in a mansion on Buckingham Road.

"Forget about living in Manhattan," my mother always told me. "Unless you want to live in a slum."

I didn't want to live in a slum. I wanted to escape from the slum I was living in.

2

Naziland

The Bakery

Let's go back to the beginning, to a late afternoon in the autumn of 1956, when the first flesh-and-blood image of the Nazis' handiwork registers in my brain, and, at the age of four, I become aware of the connection between certain people in my neighborhood and a number of things I've seen on TV— like newsreel footage of emaciated survivors in their striped uniforms, pressing against a barbed-wire fence, behind them enormous piles of naked corpses that the Nazis didn't have time to burn before they fled the advancing allied armies.

The day it happens, I'm waiting on line with my mother in N.E. Tell's bakery, on Church Avenue, and I point to a tattoo on the inner forearm of the woman working behind the counter.

"What are those numbers?" I ask as I watch the woman place a chocolate cake into a box for the customer in front of us.

"Don't point," my mother says under her breath, swatting my hand. She then bends down and whispers in my ear, "She was in Auschwitz. The Nazis gave everybody there a number."

She doesn't have to say anything more. I know that Auschwitz is a death camp—I've known that for almost as long as I've understood language. I know because everybody knows. And I know that six million Jews died in the camps—everybody knows that, too—and I know about the trains, and the slave labor, and the medical experiments, and the gas chambers, and the crematoria, and that the Nazis turned Jews into bars of soap and made their flesh into fashionable lampshades.

And now that I know about the blue numbers, I start seeing them everywhere: on the liver-spotted skin of an old man leafing through *Life* magazine in my father's candy store; on the pale forearm of a subway straphanger rumbling towards Brighton Beach; and on the flesh of a woman younger than my mother, whom I see one afternoon sitting alone on a park bench, staring blankly into the Parade Grounds.

What I don't know is how I'll ever again be able to walk into the bakery and *not* wonder how the squat, platinum-haired lady in the immaculate white uniform escaped the gas chamber, or what she must have thought as she watched the thick black smoke billow from the crematoria.

The Third Grade: 1960

"Does anybody know someone who was in a concentration camp?" our teacher, Mrs. Feinstein, asks the class during a social studies lesson.

Daniel Silver is the only one who raises his hand.

"Who do you know, Daniel?"

"My mother," he says. "She was in Dachau."

"Do you know how she survived?"

"She could split logs into three even pieces with an axe."

"Your mother has a good eye. She's *very* lucky the Nazis

found that useful."

"I know," says Daniel as I look at him from across the room, dumbfounded by what I've just heard—because I've spent dozens of afternoons at his house, and he's never said a word to me about his mother's having been in a concentration camp. Which is why, later that day, as we sit on his bedroom floor playing Monopoly, I ask him, "Why doesn't your mother have numbers on her arm?"

"Because they only gave them to Auschwitz prisoners," he says with a shrug as he counts out $200 to buy a railroad.

And that's the only time we ever speak of the camps. It doesn't even come up when I visit him that summer at the new house he's moved to near my grandmother, in Gravesend, and we spend the day sitting on the front porch with his parents, listening to the old Yiddish records his father, Sam, is playing on the phonograph.

"It's called klezmer music," Daniel tells me as his father turns up the volume for the song that's just come on—a song in which the musicians play their instruments faster and faster, until it seems as if they're playing so fast, the fiddles might catch fire. Then, as the music fades out, Daniel says, "That one's my favorite. Don't you *love* it?"

He looks at me, awaiting an answer, as his father cues up another record, and I know that I can't tell him the truth—that I hate the music, that the very sound of it fills my head with images of dead Jews lying in ghetto streets... of naked Jews trudging to gas chambers... of snarling dogs, barbed wire, soap, and lampshades...

"Oh, yeah," I finally say with some enthusiasm. "It's *really* good."

"We thought you'd like that one," says Sam Silver, with a

big smile.

So, I sit there for the rest of the afternoon, listening to him spin the hottest tunes from his extensive archive of klezmer classics. And every time I glance at Daniel's mother, Liba, sitting silently by the phonograph, swaying ever so slightly to the relentlessly ecstatic beat as she sips a glass of lemonade, I keep seeing her splitting those logs in Dachau and the SS commandos standing nearby, unable to take their eyes off the voluptuous, axe-wielding Jewess, their conflicted hearts full of murder and a feeling that I've not yet learned to call "lust." And the music just keeps playing like the soundtrack to a movie I don't want to be in, something like *The Diary of Anne Frank*—which I'd seen on TV not that long ago and found myself, like every other red-blooded Jewish boy, quite taken with the girl who wrote in notebooks.

The Beach Club: 1962

I see them in the locker room at Brighton Beach Baths—five men, about my grandfather's age, standing naked by the showers and jabbering in Yiddish. I think I'm seeing things—the men have no dicks and no balls; sparse, gray pubic hair covers the empty space between their legs.

Then I see the blue numbers, and I understand: The Nazis did it. In Auschwitz. What else could it have been?

I try to turn away, to *not* look and *not* imagine what happened to them. But I can't. I imagine all too clearly the torture, the medical experiments, the Nazi doctors slicing up screaming young men. And I wonder how anybody could have lived through such a thing, a so-called doctor cutting off your dick and balls *for no reason, probably without anesthesia.* Yet they *had* survived. There they are, right in front of me, as alive and animated as anyone, making no effort to hide their mutilations, seemingly unaware that I'm staring.

"Those guys don't have any dicks," I whisper to Barry Gardner, who's taken me as his guest to this private beach club.

"I know," he says, concentrating on tying his sneakers.

"How can you stand to look at them?"

"I don't look," he says.

But unlike Barry—whose father had changed the family name from Goldberg because he didn't want people to know they were Jewish, and with their olive complexions they looked Italian or maybe Spanish—I haven't yet learned how to *not* look at things I don't want to see. Nor have I mastered the far more difficult skill of banishing from my brain the disturbing thoughts and images that always seem to be slithering in. I haven't even learned to make myself change the channel every time another death camp survivor comes on TV to speak of the unspeakable.

Oh, I'll become numb to it all in a couple of years, and soon enough the very notion of genocidal slaughter will cease to appall me—though I'll still pretend to listen in Hebrew school when old Rabbi Schneeberg launches into another one of his stories about Auschwitz or Dachau or Treblinka or Bergen-Belsen or Buchenwald, the names that have become as familiar to me as the names of my own family. But I won't really hear what he's saying. I will have finally learned to tune things out and send my mind elsewhere, to another planet, a million miles away, where there are no death camps, and Jews are not made into bars of soap, or lampshades, or pieces of parchment on which Nazi artists have drawn serene Bavarian sunsets.

I will at last have learned to be more like my friend Barry Gardner, the secret Jew.

3

Heil Irwin!

Yes, the war had ended seven years before I was born, but that didn't mean it was over. It would never be over, not as long as the people who lived through it remained alive. World War II (along with the ghost of the Brooklyn Dodgers) lingered like a mass hallucination on East 17th Street and in large swaths of the surrounding borough. It was no longer a shooting war, of course. It was a mop-up operation, a war of words and ideas, a constant pounding of more verbal nails into the Nazi coffin, a stake through the vampire-Nazi heart, a daily confrontation with the knowledge that the Nazis weren't all dead, that some of them roamed free in South America, and that somehow the Third Reich might again rise from its ashes. Perhaps it was even a premonition that someday, after enough time had passed, certain people would begin to suggest that six million Jews were not systematically slaughtered in death camps, that it was all a big misunderstanding, a misinterpretation of history, that it was really typhus that had wiped them out, that it was an unavoidable public health catastrophe no different than the bubonic plague, and even if it wasn't, who's to say that they didn't deserve it anyway?

A day never passed when I didn't hear somebody express an opinion about the Nazis—usually my father. All you had to do to get him going was point to one of those "cute" little candy-colored Volkswagen Beetles parked on the street and say that its rear engine provided excellent traction in the snow or that you were considering buying one because the price was so reasonable.

Or if you really wanted to piss him off, you might try praising the superior quality and craftsmanship of the Mercedes-Benz, that magnificent Teutonic driving machine that had served as the official staff car of the Third Reich. A Jew (at least a Jew with half a brain in his head) would never say such a thing. It was always some goy who said it, usually while thumbing through the latest issue of *Motor Trend* in my father's candy store. And every time it happened, my father, who I'd heard (though not from him) had liberated a death camp in the final days of the war and had seen the mountains of corpses and had smelled the decaying flesh and the skeletal survivors, barely clinging to life, covered in their own filth—it was the kind of smell that never left you, my mother said—would look the ignorant bastard in the eye and say, "It's a Nazi car, schmuck." And if the schmuck continued to insist that the Mercedes was still the best-made car in the world, then my father would tell him that it was Jewish slave labor, courtesy of the concentration camps, that built VWs *and* Mercedeses. In fact, that's what he said about any product imported from the country he still called Nazi *Fucking* Germany when he thought I wasn't listening.

Yeah, we all hated the Nazis (if not necessarily their products), and if anybody didn't, he kept his fool mouth shut about it. Because if you lived in Flatbush, you were surrounded by Jews. And Jews, having paid the price in blood, now owned the

Bobby in Naziland

Nazis outright, and we could do anything we wanted to them. It was our birthright. If we felt like it, we could kidnap Nazis off the streets of Argentina, drag their arrogant Nazi asses back to Israel, and hang them from the nearest lamppost. And nobody except another Nazi would say *boo*—not to our faces, anyway. Most people, if they knew what was good for them, would pat us on the back and give us a round of applause. *Never again, motherfucker. Never again...*

Or we could take it out on Mr. Kruger, our incompetent, uncooperative super, who couldn't keep the boiler and washing machines running, couldn't keep the halls clean, and spoke English with a guttural German accent that made him sound like a cartoon Nazi.

My father called him "that damn Kraut," and the neighborhood kids, Jews and goyim alike, called his wife "Eva Braun" and him "Mister Hitler," usually as he was sullenly dragging the trashcans to the curb, which was the only job he seemed to do with any regularity.

"Sohmday, you kidz vil ged in trahbul for sayink daht" was the only thing he ever said in response.

We also routinely beat the shit out of his blond and suspiciously Aryan-looking twin sons, Walter and Karl, who were my age and had been relegated to the "dumb" class in school due to their language difficulties. Anytime we saw the twins coming down the street—they were always together—somebody would call out, "Hey Hitlers, gas any Jews lately?" or the *goyishe* variant, "Hey Hitlers, you lost the war, now you gotta pay!" Then one or more of us would pummel them with a flurry of body blows.

But Walter and Karl were pacifists and stoics to boot. They never fought back and never cried, either. They just stood there, barely defending themselves, and taking it until we stopped.

Which infuriated us even more and led to even more severe beatings—until the Krugers finally took the hint and got the hell off East 17th Street, where they didn't belong and never had a chance.

The day we found out they were moving to California, which sounded as far away as the moon, was the day we saw the movers loading up the truck with their furniture. Walter and Karl stood on the street, watching, and as word of their impending departure spread, a half-dozen of us surrounded them and, stamping our feet and clapping our hands, began chanting:

The Hitlers are moving today, today!
The Hitlers are moving today!
The Hitlers are moving today, today!
3,200 miles away...

Not only were we skilled at tormenting Nazis—or people we perceived to be Nazis, even if they happened to be refugees themselves, as the Krugers probably were—but we knew how to laugh at Nazis, too, because laughter was "the best medicine," at least according to *Reader's Digest*. Which is to say that I lived among the people who would one day comprise the core audience for *The Producers*, both the movie and the Broadway musical—written by *Jewish* Mel Brooks, né Kaminsky, from Williamsburg—and who'd watch *Dr. Strangelove*—directed by *Jewish* Stanley Kubrick from the Bronx—every time it was on TV, just to see the bit at the end when Strangelove rises from his wheelchair and tells the president, "*Mein Führer*, I can walk!"

The snapshot in our family photo album of my father giving the Nazi salute while wearing a Nazi uniform he'd taken off a POW—captioned "Heil Irwin!" in my mother's immaculate script—cracked me up every time I saw it, too. I loved that picture even more than the 8-by-10 of my father clad in his American combat fatigues, crouched behind a machine gun, looking like the comic-book character Sergeant Rock blasting away at some unseen enemy.

But just as my father refused to talk to me about the death camp he'd liberated, he also refused to talk about his war wound, and it was my mother who had to tell me that he'd gotten "hit in the *tushie*" with a piece of shrapnel, in France, and earned a Purple Heart for his trouble. When I asked my father to show me his medal, he claimed, incomprehensibly, that he'd never bothered to collect it.

Nor could I find any mention of his war wound or Purple Heart in our well-worn (and gruesomely illustrated) copy of the *History of the Ninety-Fourth Infantry Division*, which I spent hours poring over, looking in vain for my father's name. Yet, I still found it extraordinary that there existed a book—an actual *hardcover book* that had a direct connection to something my father had done—and that the 94th Division logo embossed on the book's cover looked exactly like the old 94th Division patch he kept in a jewelry box in his bedroom closet.

His other war souvenirs he'd stashed in the foyer closet, in a musty-smelling canvas bag that I'd dig out on weekend mornings, spreading its contents across my bedroom floor so I could play with the most concrete evidence I possessed that my father really had fought the Nazis. The bag contained one razor-sharp American bayonet; one ceremonial ivory-handled Nazi bayonet in a golden sheath that looked identical to the sword that had graced the cover of a recent *Saga* magazine; one Nazi helmet; one pair of Nazi field glasses; one Nazi compass (which looked like an American compass except for the 0 designating

Ost, the German word for East, and which my father said worked better than an American compass); and one quilted white box with an embossed gold seal of the United States. Inside that box were my father's dog tags, which displayed his name, serial number, and blood type, O+. The box also contained a small Nazi flag and his collection of Nazi civilian medals—a few dozen dull-gray pieces of tin decorated with swastikas and stylized Nazi eagles—doled out for things like motherhood, industrial production, and growing wheat, as my mother explained to me because my father wouldn't. Though he did say that a POW had given him the medals in exchange for a pack of cigarettes.

I pretended they were the medals my father had won but never collected—his Purple Heart and the various European campaign decorations that some 50 years later the Veterans Administration would finally bestow upon him after tracking him down in his Florida retirement village. And I'd pin these Nazi baubles to my pajamas, go into the bathroom and, ignoring the swastikas, admire my bemedaled self in the mirror, thinking how I couldn't wait to fight in a war and kill whoever needed killing so I could earn my own real medals and wear them proudly on my chest.

My father told me that he had also brought a German Luger home from the war but had sold it to a collector just before I was born because my mother didn't want a gun in the house—a perfectly rational decision that filled me with profound disappointment. I'd have given anything to be able to play with a real German Luger rather than my German Luger water pistol, because I was a kid who loved guns and loved war. I loved the very idea of war, the glory of war, the medal-earning opportunities it presented. And I loved my battalion of toy soldiers, tanks, artillery, jeeps, planes, and armored personnel carriers that I'd set up in a Maginot Line across the Western Front of my bedroom.

Bobby in Naziland

And I loved my arsenal of noise-making and cap-shooting rifles, pistols, and automatic weapons—though I'd have much preferred the real thing. And I loved to play soldier, decked out in a full complement of Nazi accessories—helmet, ceremonial bayonet, compass, field glasses, and medals—because they were *real*, and who wants to play with toys when you've got the real thing, even if the people they once belonged to were known to have decorated their homes with Jewskin lampshades?

"How many Nazis did you kill in the war, Dad?" was another question my father refused to answer to my satisfaction, no matter how many times I asked him.

"Nobody," he always said, but I kept asking because his answer always left me wondering how it was possible for anybody to have fought in World War II and not to have killed at least *one* Nazi. And I didn't understand why anybody, especially my father, would lie to me about *not* killing Nazis. Wasn't killing Nazis a good thing to do, something to be proud of?

Decades later, as he lay dying in a Florida hospital, my father told me a story I'd never heard before: In Czechoslovakia, at the end of the war, he was assigned to a POW camp because his commanding officer thought it was a good idea to have Jewish soldiers guarding Nazi prisoners—with orders to shoot on sight anyone who tried to escape. And he was an ideal Jew for the job because, being fluent in Yiddish—essentially a German dialect written in Hebrew characters—he understood a lot of German.

His first day in the camp, he overheard two prisoners talking about him. They thought he was a raw recruit, and they wanted to see what "the Jew" would do if they acted as if they were going to escape.

"He's not going to shoot us," one prisoner told the other in

German, motioning towards my father.

They both began walking towards the perimeter fence.

My father, as instructed, cocked the bolt of his carbine and took aim at the "escaping" Nazis, who, realizing they were about to be shot on the spot, stopped dead in their tracks and put up their hands.

"Don't mess with him," the other prisoner said. "We made it this far. He'll kill us."

The matter-of-fact way my father told this story, apropos of nothing, as if he were just imparting some useful information that had suddenly popped into his head, left me with the impression that in the course of his military career he'd killed lots of Nazis, that doing so was just another chore, like taking out the garbage—business as usual, in other words, a necessary fact of war. And I wondered if this was finally an oblique answer to the question I'd asked him so many times, so many years ago. And if it was, why had he waited 45 years to answer it? Did he feel that he was about to meet some of those young German soldiers he'd so long ago dispatched into the Great Beyond? Was he trying to clear his conscience? Is that what war is really about? You kill people because it's your job, and it haunts you for the rest of your life, even if the people you killed were Nazis and Jew-hating war criminals whose atrocities you'd witnessed firsthand?

He died before I had a chance to ask him.

4

Tales of Eichmann

That I wanted to be a Nazi hunter when I grew up isn't surprising. Nor is it surprising that I'd taken the trouble to find out that if I *really* wanted to hunt Nazis, then I'd have to move to Israel and join the Mossad, the "Jewish CIA," whose "covert operatives" had, for years, been searching for fugitives from the Third Reich in every corner of Argentina, Brazil, and Paraguay, those exotic South American countries that had welcomed with open arms Nazi war criminals, like Adolf Eichmann.

Eichmann, my mother told me, was, along with Josef Mengele, the Nazi "doctor," one of the two most wanted Nazis on earth. She also said that she hated Eichmann even more than Mengele because it was Eichmann who'd organized the "Final Solution," and it was Eichmann who'd built the extermination camps and developed the insidious gassing techniques, which were responsible for the deaths of one million Jews at Auschwitz alone. And since most sane people agreed that Hitler had blown out his brains in the bunker in the final days of the war, she'd transferred her hatred of *der Führer* to Eichmann, whom she now held personally responsible for everything having to do with the Holocaust.

So inflamed was my imagination with my mother's tales of Eichmann, he'd become something of my personal bogeyman, the swastika-spangled Gestapo monster lurking under my bed. Which is probably why, when I returned home from school on the afternoon of May 23, 1960, my mother, in a state of extreme excitement, announced that they'd captured Eichmann in Argentina. She then practically dragged me into the kitchen so we could listen to the radio, where an announcer, reading from the latest update, was describing him as "a logistics specialist."

The precise meaning of this term became clear to me over the course of the afternoon: Adolf Eichmann, *Obersturmbannführer* of the Final Solution, had figured out the most efficient ways to round up Jews and transport them to concentration camps, where they'd be selected for slave labor and death, medical experiments and death, or just death. That's why every Jew I knew, especially the Jews in my own house, couldn't wait to see the Nazi bastard hang—the sooner the better—to make a point: The world needed to know that you did not fuck with the Jews, not anymore. 'Cause the Jews were a vengeful people with biblical memories, and whatever you did to them, they were going to find a way to make you pay... in spades... even if it took 5,000 years. And capturing Eichmann had taken a mere 15, which might have been two lifetimes for me, but for my parents and a lot of other people, it must have seemed as if the Holocaust had happened only yesterday.

The blood lust was palpable.

In the year 2000, long after everybody had stopped paying attention, the Israeli government quietly declassified the story of a half-Jewish Dachau "political prisoner" whom the Gestapo had beaten to near-blindness before releasing him on the eve of World War II. This obscure man, in 1961, had tried to speak out about his role in capturing the "Dybbuk"—demon—Eichmann's code-name. But his lack of discretion succeeded only in infuriating the almighty Mossad—who, according to the Argentine newspaper *El Imparcial*, promptly accused him of being none other than Josef Mengele and, in a joint operation with the BND, the West German intelligence agency, arrested him in Argentina and tortured him for 15 days. Then, after an analysis of his fingerprints showed that he was *not* Mengele, they let him go.

I mention this improbable tale now because it's the missing piece that cries out to be more than a historical footnote to a nearly forgotten incident, and because it changes the very essence of what everybody thought they knew about how Israeli intelligence agents had managed to snatch Adolf Eichmann off a Buenos Aires street and spirit him back to Jerusalem to stand trial for crimes against humanity.

What I didn't know in 1960—and still wouldn't had I not decided to compare my memory of Eichmann's capture to the historical record—was that this political prisoner, Lothar Hermann, in 1938, right after *Kristallnacht*, had fled with his wife to Argentina. There he chose to conceal his Jewish identity, even from his daughter, Silvia, who was born a few years later. Indeed, she was so oblivious of her heritage that, in 1956, now a teenager, she began dating Eichmann's son Klaus, whom she'd met at a local movie theatre that was showing a German film. Klaus used his real family name (which meant nothing to Silvia) because his father insisted that he do so.

Equally oblivious of the implications of his own Aryan heritage, Klaus Eichmann came to the Hermanns' house and over soft drinks in their parlor—evidently unaware of the ongoing war-crime trials in Germany—bragged about how his dad was a high-ranking Gestapo officer, blithely telling the Hermanns that the one mistake the Nazis had made was that they'd failed to exterminate all the Jews. As it happened, Lothar Hermann, who could barely believe what his ears were hearing, had just read, with his deteriorating eyesight, an article about the trials in a German-language weekly, *Argentinisches Tageblatt*, which mentioned Adolf Eichmann as one of the numerous Nazi war criminals still at large, most likely in South America.

Hermann realized that the time had come to tell Silvia the truth—that he was half-Jewish, and that that was among the reasons (he was also a socialist) the Nazis had sent him to Dachau. After breaking the news to his astonished daughter, he mailed a letter to the German prosecutor's office, in Frankfurt, saying that he thought he knew where Eichmann was. Several months later, one of the prosecutors, Fritz Bauer, himself a concentration camp survivor, wrote back, asking Hermann if he and Silvia would act as spies and gather more information.

They agreed to do so, in part because there was a $10,000 reward on Eichmann's head—a sizeable fortune in Argentina in 1956 (though Hermann would have to wait until 1972 before the Israeli government grudgingly cut him a check).

Silvia's first act of espionage was to ask Klaus for his address, which he gave to her: 14 Garibaldi Street. The dark-haired beauty then paid an unannounced visit to Casa Eichmann, an isolated cottage on a run-down, dimly lit block in the Bancalari district of Buenos Aires. A middle-aged man answered the door, introduced himself as Klaus's uncle, Ricardo Klement, invited her into the ramshackle house, and chatted with her about her schoolwork as they waited for Klaus to return home. When he walked in, about an hour later, he greeted Klement as "Father." That was when Silvia realized her charming host was indeed Adolf *Fucking* Eichmann, mastermind of the Final Solution.

Which is where the Hermanns are erased from the picture and the "official" story kicks in—the one that my mother could never stop talking about, the one I watched on TV, read about in the newspapers, and listened to on the radio... the one that old Rabbi Schneeberg taught us in Hebrew school as if it were a Bible story.

Days after the capture, acting as if a highly placed source in the Mossad were feeding him juicy details, unknown to all but an exclusive inner circle, the rabbi told us how the Mossad (apparently having received the information clairvoyantly) had set up shop on Garibaldi Street, put Eichmann under 24-hour surveillance, trailed him around the city, and taken surreptitious photographs, which they then compared to the photos in his SS file. Plastic surgeons, the rabbi said, had done extensive work on Eichmann's face but hadn't touched his ears, and it was the shape of his ears that convinced the Mossad, beyond all reasonable doubt, that Adolf Eichmann and the man who called himself Ricardo Klement were the same person.

He told us how at 7:40 p.m., on May 11, 1960—four years after Klaus Eichmann's anti-Semitic rants had originally aroused Lothar Hermann's suspicions (a minor detail the rabbi left out because, like everybody else, he didn't know)—two Mossad agents, pretending to be fixing a car down the block from Eichmann's house, waited for him to return from his job as a foreman at a Mercedes-Benz factory.

He told us how they saw him step off his usual bus and walk towards them down the dark street.

He told us how, as Eichmann walked past, one of the agents

asked him, "Got a cigarette?"

A ripple of laughter spread through the class, and when it subsided, the rabbi told us that as Eichmann stopped and reached into his pocket, a third agent, parked in a nearby car, switched on the high beams, momentarily blinding the former Gestapo colonel. In that split second, the rabbi said, the first two Mossad agents jumped Eichmann, and one of the agents would later recall that the most wanted Nazi war criminal on earth emitted "the primal cry of a cornered animal" before they could knock him unconscious with a karate chop to the back of the neck.

For three days, the rabbi said, the agents interrogated Eichmann at a Buenos Aires safe house, and for three days he refused to admit who he was. Then, Rabbi Schneeberg continued, at the end of the third day, his will broken, he confessed: "I am Adolf Eichmann. That is indeed my name." He told us that Eichmann then asked for a glass of wine, but the agents instead injected him with a dose of tranquilizers "big enough to knock out a horse."

Again the rabbi waited for the laughter to cease before he explained how the Mossad dressed the unconscious fugitive in the uniform of the Israeli national airline, El Al, brought him to the airport, told immigration officials that he was a sick employee, and strapped him into a first-class seat on the next flight to Tel Aviv—at which point the Bible class burst into spontaneous applause.

The rabbi, of course, had gotten this information from the New York newspapers. It was on every front page, and when I stopped by my father's candy store after Hebrew school that day, the crowd that had gathered on the sidewalk were reading all about it.

Bobby in Naziland

The *New York Times* headline above a photo of Eichmann, resplendent in his SS uniform, said it all: "Israel Seizes Nazi Chief of Extermination of Jews."

As I walked into the store, a man, about 70, a survivor with the blue numbers tattooed on his arm, was paying for his copy of the *Daily News.* "Just hang the son of a bitch *now*," he said to my father.

"Better idea," said Moskowitz, one of the candy store regulars, looking up from the *Herald Tribune* he'd spread across the top of the ice cream freezer. "How about they just burn him alive?"

"No," said Cohen, another long-time customer, "keep him in a cage so we can go there and spit on him."

A couple of guys loitering in the back of the store, near the rack with the dirty books, greeted these suggestions with a round of raucous hoots.

So jubilant was everybody's mood, you'd never have guessed that beyond Flatbush, much of the world was less than pleased with this miraculous turn of events. Nobody was talking about how, as I'd discover decades later, Argentina was demanding that Israel return Eichmann. Nor did I hear anybody mention that other newspapers, outside New York, had condemned the kidnapping as "jungle law," implying that the Israelis were no different than the Nazis.

All I knew was what I heard at home, in school, and in the store: The Jews finally got the Nazi bastard and it was about fucking time. And Israel, in total agreement, charged Eichmann with 15 counts of crimes against humanity, crimes against the Jewish people, and war crimes. Then, one year later, intent on serving up a little justice Jewish-style, they put him on trial in Jerusalem.

Every night at seven, for months on end, my mother watched

the trial unfold on *The Huntley-Brinkley Report*. Sometimes I joined her, and what I saw on TV was a man with a receding hairline, wearing a pair of thick, black-rimmed eyeglasses and a dark suit and tie, sitting, for his own protection, in a bulletproof-glass booth between two guards, and listening on a pair of headphones to a simultaneous translation of the proceedings. No matter how hard I tried, I couldn't reconcile the mass-murdering SS colonel, who'd lurked in my imagination for as long as I'd known what a Nazi was, with this bland-looking specimen of humanity who bore a slight resemblance to my uncle Herb. Adolf Eichmann just didn't look the part—neither evil nor dashing nor even *Nazi*. And yet... whoever and whatever he was, he did appear to have a huge pair of balls—*chutzpa*, as people were calling it.

Stoic, even indifferent, throughout the trial, he seemed unconcerned (or unaware) that he was surrounded by Jews who, given half a chance, would have ripped off those big Nazi balls with their bare hands and shoved them down his Nazi throat. Eichmann didn't show any emotion even when he listened to the testimony of 99 concentration camp survivors who described an assortment of abominations for which they held him personally responsible—one former inmate recalled how he was forced to pile thousands of corpses in pyramidal heaps, burn them, extract the gold fillings from their teeth, grind up the bones with a bone-grinding machine built expressly to obliterate all evidence of genocide, and then eat lunch on top of the remaining corpses because there was no place else to sit.

When he told his side of the story, Eichmann—soon to be held up as the quintessential example of the "banality of evil"—still seemed utterly impassive. He was a man of little power, he said, who was only "following orders" and doing his job, which was merely to transmit the instructions of *der Führer*, Adolf Hitler.

Bobby in Naziland

But it didn't matter what he said or how he said it. The truth had been established beyond a shadow of a doubt: Eichmann loved gassing Jews and he was good at it. Yet even when the three-judge panel found him guilty of all 15 counts and sentenced him to hang, he did nothing more than stand quietly in the glass booth, looking as if he were listening to somebody give him directions to the nearest bus stop.

I didn't understand how this Nazi could so calmly accept his fate, how a man sentenced to hang could act as if nothing had happened. Did he not believe they'd really do it? Or was it a demonstration of the Aryan pride I'd heard so much about, of Nazi courage in the face of death? Or maybe he was just a war criminal who knew he had it coming, knew there was nothing he could do about it, and probably considered himself lucky that they weren't going to slow-roast him over an open flame with an apple in his mouth... like a "Pigjew."

I listened to the execution on the kitchen radio, beamed in live by satellite from Jerusalem. It was May 31, 1962, a Thursday evening in Brooklyn, just before midnight in Israel.

My mother, who believed in divine retribution, was standing by the sink and smoking a cigarette as she washed dishes. "Oh, just get it over with," she muttered, as if she were afraid they might call the whole thing off.

I remember that more clearly than the broadcast. In fact, the only detail I can recall is that as Eichmann stood on the gallows, the announcer said, he asked the warden to loosen the ropes that bound his knees. And I thought, Who cares if the ropes are too tight? He's going to be dead in a minute.

A half-century-old *New York Times* story confirms that my memory is accurate. Eichmann did ask the warden to loosen the ropes binding his knees, and the warden ordered a prison official to do so. I remember reading that article—"Eichmann Dies on Gallows for Role in Killing of Jews"—in the candy store the next day, enthralled by the gothicly pornographic detail: Eichmann in his holding cell, in fog-shrouded Ramle Prison, drinking his last "meal," a bottle of Israeli wine, after his final appeal for mercy is denied. Two prison officials then bring him to the execution chamber, lead him up the stairway to the gallows. He refuses the traditional black hood. The warden then places the noose around his neck. Standing erect, maintaining his famous Aryan composure to the bitter end, Eichmann says, "I am ready," and then spouts his last words, some stupid Nazi horseshit about war, flag, and country. Three executioners then simultaneously pull three levers—only one of which is the real lever—and the Gestapo colonel vanishes down the black trap door. His body is cremated in a special furnace, and his ashes are scattered in the Mediterranean, outside Israeli territorial waters.

As I read that last detail on my computer, in the 21st century, again I see myself in the kitchen with my mother on that faraway Brooklyn evening, but now I can hear the reporter relay that very last bit of news about Eichmann's ashes, talking over the background sound of a helicopter hovering high above the wine-dark sea.

5

Reading for Pleasure

Adolf Eichmann was still cooling his heels in Ramle Prison the morning my eye fell upon a swastika on the spine of a book that somebody had stashed on a high shelf in the foyer bookcase. Climbing up on a chair, I took the book down, and I knew even before I opened it that somewhere in this encyclopedia-size volume I'd find the answers to questions I'd been wondering about for a long time.

Reptilian instinct alone guided me to the relevant entries in an index I could barely navigate. And when I turned to the designated pages, I did indeed locate passages so vividly appalling that when I reread them today they seem just as ghastly as they did the day I first laid eyes on them, as an eight-year-old, ambitiously making the transition from *Fun with Dick and Jane* to the most recent arrival from the Book of the Month Club, *The Rise and Fall of the Third Reich*, by William Shirer—a transition I worked at countless mornings, sitting with the book on my bedroom floor, reading "the good parts" over and over, until they burnt an indelible impression into my impressionable brain, and taught me *Reading = Physical Pleasure* of the sort I'd never found in any book; not even the Tom Swift and Hardy Boys series, which I'd discover the following year, would come close.

How is it possible, I wondered, that this somber-looking 1,245-page tome could contain tales so electrifyingly macabre that my body practically vibrated as I read them? One passage described Nazi guards observing writhing masses of naked flesh through gas-chamber peepholes, men and women together, shrieking and gasping for air as they choked to death on Zyklon B.

But Shirer's account of a "medical" experiment the Nazis themselves had meticulously documented provided an even greater jolt of Eros/Thanatos-style thrills: Naked men were put outside in sub-zero temperatures and doused with cold water every hour until they stopped screaming. Then, on the verge of death, they were brought inside so Nazi doctors could conduct "warming experiments"—from which they concluded that the best way to thaw out a frozen man was to put him in bed with one or more naked women, and let the women's body heat warm him as they had "intercourse." The doctors also determined through repeated testing that one naked woman unthawed a man faster than two, because, they deduced, a "chilled man" and one woman were both less inhibited and clung more closely to each other during the sexual act.

I didn't know that some people might call such material "Nazi porn," similar to what was only hinted at in the more lurid men's magazines of the day, the ones that featured so-called "true" stories like "The Last Days of Hitler's Depraved Nazi Nymphos." I only knew that I was reading a book that I shouldn't be reading, a book that I'd never tell anybody I'd read, a book that I did not want my parents to catch me reading, and a book that I wanted to read every morning until I had my fill of whatever it was the book was filling me with.

Bobby in Naziland

Nineteen years would pass before another book about the Nazis would make an impression upon me as profound as that of *The Rise and Fall of the Third Reich.*

That a novel dealing with the Holocaust would one day be set in Flatbush was probably inevitable. But who could have predicted that it would be written not by a Jew or even a native Flatbushian, but by a goy from Newport News, Virginia, who had lived in the neighborhood for only a few months and was so ignorant of Jewish customs that the sight of men walking around in yarmulkes provoked him to write a letter to his father asking why people were wearing "funny hats."

The goy in question, William Styron, did his time in Flatbush in 1949, and he wandered through this "exotic" neighborhood with eyes so fresh and innocent, he was able to see it for what it was and express a simple truth that I'd never before heard anyone say: Flatbush was more Jewish than Tel Aviv.

Styron's southern perspective also enabled him to see something I had been seeing every day from the moment I was born but had never paid any attention to: the intimacy with which concentration camp survivors and army vets who'd fought the Nazis commingled with the ghosts of the Holocaust.

At least that's how it struck me when I read *Sophie's Choice,* set in 1947. In the pages of that book, I saw the old neighborhood through Styron's gentile eyes as his alter ego, Stingo—the ultimate Flatbush outsider—took me on a grand tour of the streets I knew better than any streets on the planet. Stingo/Styron shopped for groceries where my mother shopped for groceries, in the sawdust-strewn aisles of the A&P on Church Avenue. And he drank his liquor at the Maple Court Tavern's horseshoe-shaped bar, that funky Church Avenue dive where my friend Brian Riley's stepfather could be found on any given afternoon, knocking back his highballs and whisky shots. And Stingo/Styron picnicked in a place that I practically lived in, albeit cautiously, once the Puerto Rican incident had faded from my parents' memory and they again permitted me to venture there by myself: Prospect Park.

In the book's first paragraph, Stingo describes himself as a "lonesome young Southerner... self-exiled to Flatbush... wandering amid the Kingdom of the Jews." He then talks about the enormous house, which he calls the "Pink Palace," where he (and Styron) lived.

It was a house I knew well, except by the time I came to know it, it was neither pink nor a palace. It was the decrepit rooming house on the corner of Caton Avenue and Marlborough Road— across the street from my nearly 100 percent Jewish grade school, PS 249, which hadn't yet been built during Styron's brief Brooklyn sojourn. Stingo's upstairs neighbor in that house was the Sophie of the title—Sophie Zawistowska, an Auschwitz survivor who was Catholic rather than Jewish (a "Polack" as she'd have been known in the neighborhood) but had the blue numbers tattooed on her forearm just the same. Though (as I'd later learn) there really was such a young woman living upstairs from Styron in the rooming house, for all I knew as I was reading the book, Sophie could have been the fictional incarnation of any number of my neighbors, perhaps even the woman who worked in the bakery, three stores down from my father's candy store— the platinum-blonde lady in the immaculate white uniform on whose muscular forearm I saw tattooed those blue numbers late one afternoon in the autumn of 1956.

Because when Stingo/Styron first emerged from the Church Avenue subway station "one fine day in June," and made his way to the Pink Palace, he'd have passed a candy store attached to the train station (where my father and grandfather had recently set up shop), a trolley car stop (which would become a bus stop in 1956), a five-and-dime store, and Pizzello the shoemaker, before walking past N.E. Tell's bakery. And one would assume that when Styron, like every other Flatbushian, returned to Tell's for his daily ration of freshly baked bread, he couldn't help but stare at the blue numbers on the bakery lady's arm, just as I did, and just as Stingo did when he saw them on Sophie's arm. And how could he not wonder, as every Flatbushian with eyes must have wondered at some point: *Good God, how many people in this neighborhood were in Auschwitz?*

I walked past the Pink Palace twice every day for seven years, on my way to and from school, and every time I did, I felt its "bad vibrations," as Styron called them in the book, the vibrations that told him there was "something subtly and inexplicably wrong" in the house.

Yet, I never spoke of the house... to anyone. Somehow, I felt that it wasn't meant to be spoken of. And I don't recall anybody else ever talking about the house, either, even my classmates who lived on the same block and must have been aware of its weird energy, just as I was. I didn't even know it was a rooming house. I had no idea what it was. The house was just *there*, the great unspoken blot of decay in the midst of neatly trimmed lawns and well-maintained private homes—a gray hulk in desperate need of a paint job (of any color), its front yard little more than a tangle of weeds and clumps of dirt.

Sometimes I saw people coming and going from the house— never kids, always slightly seedy-looking adults, the kind of people you'd see drinking in the Maple Court Tavern—an ever-shifting parade of boarders, though I didn't know they were boarders. Occasionally on a warm spring day I'd see them sitting by open windows on the upper floors, looking out at Caton Avenue and the Parade Grounds across the street, and as I hurried by, I'd cast a furtive glance in their direction.

If anybody was aware that an author of some acclaim had once lived in that house, and in his rented room had begun writing his first book, *Lie Down in Darkness*—Stingo describes a parallel experience in *Sophie's Choice*—they kept it to themselves. No historical plaque had been affixed to the side of the Pink Palace, and William Styron, unlike William Shirer, was not a name that could be found in our bookcase or a name that my achievement-worshipping mother had ever uttered in my presence—because Styron was a goy who hadn't yet written about Jews or the Holocaust. That's what kept him off her radar screen, the one on which she kept tabs on famous and otherwise significant Jews of all stripes, even those who'd changed their names to hide their Jewishness, and "pass," as she called it, like Tony Curtis, formerly Bernard Schwartz—How did she know this? Was there a secret list?—and the Gardners, formerly the Goldbergs, significant Jews only because they lived across the street and my good friend Barry Gardner sometimes took me with him to Brighton Beach Baths.

And though my mother much preferred that I join her in her worship of Jews who achieved their fame by being smart and successful, like Albert Einstein and Jonas Salk, whose polio vaccine she considered a near-biblical miracle that delivered her from the mortal dread of seeing her only son wind up in an iron lung, she didn't hesitate to bring to my attention any Jew whose name wound up in the newspapers, even if it was for the crime of passing atomic bomb secrets to the Soviet Union.

6

Magical Thinking

Every time she told me the story of Julius and Ethel Rosenberg, she seemed to fixate on the same two facts—that my dead grandfather was *Julius* Rosen and that the *Rosen*bergs had a son *Robert*, who was just a little older than I was.

And though my mother usually didn't dwell on the horrific details of Julius's and Ethel's deaths, I knew from the time I was five that they'd been electrocuted at Sing Sing prison a month before my first birthday—the first husband and wife ever to be executed in the United States.

That's why the specters of Robert Rosenberg and his brother, Michael, were regular visitors as I lay in bed at night trying to fall asleep. I kept seeing them on the night of their parents' executions, looking just as they did in the picture taken that day—the one that ran in all the newspapers. Robert, in the foreground, with his big, dark, haunted eyes, looking as sad as I always did in pictures. And I'd think about how helpless and abandoned they both must have felt. Which probably explains why, just as with Eichmann, I needed to find out everything I could about how the Rosenbergs died, and I developed a kind of sixth sense for unearthing any scrap of information lurking in old magazines and encyclopedia yearbooks that might shed some light on the subject.

I learned enough about what happened in the Sing Sing death chamber on the night of June 19, 1953, that had you asked me about the double electrocution when I was, say, nine, I could have told you that according to witnesses both Rosenbergs—who looked as if they could have been my cousins from the Bronx—went to the electric chair with astonishing composure. I could have told you that a clean-shaven Julius Rosenberg walked slowly, behind a rabbi, into the glaringly lit, white-walled room as the rabbi recited the 23rd Psalm, "The Lord is my Shepherd..."—the same prayer that Mrs. Ortiz, who taught fifth grade, read in assembly at PS 249 every Friday morning. I could have told you that Rosenberg seemed to sway from side to side as he approached the brown oaken chair. And I could have told you that, at 8:06 p.m., three 2,000-volt jolts of electricity ended his life quietly, or as quietly as somebody can go when being roasted alive.

I could have told you that Ethel Rosenberg went to her death wearing a dark green print dress with white polka dots, cloth slippers, and close-cropped hair so that the electrodes could come in full contact with her skull. I could have told you that as she reached the chair where her husband had died moments earlier, she kissed a prison matron lightly on the cheek as the rabbi recited Psalms 15 ("Who shall dwell in thy holy hill? He that walketh uprightly") and 31 ("Have mercy upon me O Lord for I am in trouble"). And I could have told you that the same eyewitnesses described her execution as the more gruesome of the two. When doctors determined that Ethel's heart was still beating after the first surge of electricity, the executioner had to give her three additional jolts, causing smoke to rise from her head, float up to the ceiling, and linger in the death chamber. And I could have told you that the doctors pronounced her dead at 8:16 p.m.

What I couldn't have explained in 1961 was why I was obsessed not only with the Rosenbergs, Eichmann, and Nazi gas chambers, but with all manner of executions. Nor could I have explained why I knew more about execution techniques than anybody would have considered normal or healthy for a kid my age or any other age, or why I'd memorized the method of capital punishment used in every state in the union—information I found in the ever-helpful *Information Please Almanac*. I learned that in Wyoming and California they gassed you with cyanide (which I also knew, about California, from watching Susan Hayward go to the gas chamber in *I Want to Live*); in Florida and Pennsylvania they fried you in the electric chair; in Kansas and Delaware they hanged you; and in Utah they let you choose between hanging or a firing squad—and most people chose the firing squad, as I thought I would were I ever to be convicted of murder in Utah.

But nobody ever asked me about these things, so I kept the information to myself. Though I wanted to learn more about certain executions, I knew that if I were to ask my mother, "Why did it take so much electricity to kill Ethel Rosenberg?," she'd have gotten upset and refused to answer.

So, instead, I plied her with more general questions like: "How did the gas chamber at Auschwitz work?" This she apparently considered legitimate intellectual inquiry, and in response she'd dig out an old copy of *Life* magazine and show me a picture of the gas chamber, and tell me about Zyklon B—how it suffocated you like cyanide. Or if something about the death camps was on TV, she'd call me into the living room so I could watch it with her. And since I found fascinating all things Nazi, especially their machinery of mass extermination, I'd sit there spellbound.

But then I'd have to stop myself from peppering her with pesky follow-up questions like: "How many people could you fit in the gas chamber?" or "How long did it take them to die?" or "Did it hurt a lot?" Because those questions would be met with the same answer I'd been getting since I asked her, when I was four: "How deep do they bury you when you die?"

"I don't know," my mother had said, adding, "and you're too young to be asking questions like that."

Which is pretty much what she told me when I was six and asked if I could go to a funeral, anybody's funeral—because I wanted to see a dead person.

No, I couldn't go to a funeral, she said—because I was too young.

"But what does a dead person look like?"

"Like they're asleep," she said. "Now stop asking questions like that."

I stopped asking questions like that when, about a month later, as we were driving back from Poughkeepsie, the highway traffic slowed to a crawl as rubberneckers gawked at two cars, now crumpled, that had had a head-on collision. A man, thrown from one of the cars, was sprawled on the median, not moving, his head twisted at an unnatural angle, his eyes wide open; a woman and child were standing next to him, crying. The man didn't look like he was asleep. He looked dead. And for the rest of the trip, I kept thinking about how an accident like that could happen to anybody, even me, and how when that dead man had gotten up in the morning, he hadn't known he would be dead in a couple of hours.

Maybe I was a morbid kid or had a touch of Asperger's or was just drawn to death by a sense of taboo—I wanted to know about things I wasn't supposed to know about. And while my mother was willing, even eager, to talk to me about the mass exterminations of the Holocaust (up to a point), my parents, especially my father, refused to talk to me about death when it was real and personal—and this most likely explains what became of Johnny Banks, the only person I ever met who'd fought in the war alongside my father.

Banks, who like my father was in his mid-30s at the time, came to visit us one night in the autumn of 1959. As he and my father sat at the kitchen table, calling General Patton a "sonuvabitch," and talking about how "friggin' cold" it was at the Battle of the Bulge, my father suddenly said to him, "Go ahead, Johnny, show the kid what happened to you."

Banks hesitated for a moment. Then he grabbed his left index finger and did something I thought was a good magic trick—so good that I burst out laughing. Then he did it a second time, and it registered: With a twist, he'd removed the top two joints of his finger.

"Don't be afraid," he said, offering me his fake finger. "You can touch it."

The prothesis struck me as more of a Halloween gag than a replacement for a dismembered body part, which must be why I didn't feel revulsion as I took it from him. Normally, I couldn't bear to even think about anything having to do with lost appendages; I'd run out of the room if a medical show came on TV that had a story line about amputations, as such shows, especially *Dr. Kildare*, often did. In fact, ever since I'd seen a one-legged kid running around on crutches at a public swimming pool, his stump sticking out of his bathing suit, my dreams were filled with images of bizarre machines slicing off my own legs.

And my mother didn't help matters any by repeatedly telling

me the "inspirational" story of her uncle Jacob, a professional violinist by day who worked nights as a fabric cutter. "The night before his wedding," she said, "he fell asleep at the cutting machine, and it sliced off his right hand. He couldn't play the violin anymore, so he started his own fabric company and now he's a *millionaire!*"

The story sickened me every time I heard it, and I was just glad that Jacob lived in California, because I never wanted to meet him... or anybody else who'd had a body part sliced off.

So I was amazed by my own composure as I examined Johnny Banks's artificial digit, turning it every which way and marveling at its lifelike qualities.

"It feels like a real finger," I told him.

"Not exactly," he said. "It's cooler."

He meant there was no body heat; the finger was room temperature.

"I can't tell the difference," I said, handing him his finger and watching him screw it back into place.

He left a few hours later, and it was only then that I noticed how frail he looked. He walked with my father down the long foyer towards the door, his snow-white hair contrasting weirdly with my father's crown of jet black that contained not a strand of gray. Several years later it occurred to me that Johnny Banks, or "Johnny Finger" as I came to think of him, must have died, probably not long after his visit. I think the purpose of that visit was to say goodbye to my father—because that was the only time I ever saw Banks, and never again did I hear anything more about him, which is typical of how my father, who wouldn't even look at pictures of dead relatives, dealt with death. He refused to acknowledge it and hoped it would go away, acting as if people weren't really dead as long as you didn't say they were dead, and

Bobby in Naziland

admitting only reluctantly that death, especially the inevitability of his own, was a consequence of the human condition. That's probably how he stayed sane during those three years he spent on the front lines of a war that resulted in the deaths of some 60 million people, many of whom, I suspect, were obliterated before his very eyes.

Yes, it was magical thinking, but it had gotten him this far. And it does explain why my parents rarely told me when somebody in the family had died. They both seemed to believe, magically, that I wouldn't notice that people I'd known my entire life were suddenly no longer around. But of course I noticed, and when I asked them about these disappearances—"Where's Cousin Hymie?"—it was usually my mother who said, "He died, but we didn't want to upset you."

Which made death seem even more taboo than sex.

Yet it was my mother who'd gotten me interested in the first place, reading to me, from the time I was four, the poems of Edgar Allen Poe, whose infectious rhymes and rhythms made death seem like an absolute funhouse. How could I *not* fall under the spell of those repeating lines in "Annabel Lee," about a man burying his beautiful, prematurely dead lover in a "sepulcher by the sea," or of the repeating word "nevermore" in "The Raven," spoken by that taunting bird to a man who wants to reunite in heaven with his (again) prematurely dead lover, Lenore (which to my mother must have sounded almost as if it were her own name, Eleanor)? And it wasn't just Poe's death-obsessed verse she read to me. There was also that World War I poem "In Flanders Fields," where "poppies grow between the crosses row by row" and the (again) prematurely dead, killed in combat "short days ago" but unable to rest in peace, urge the living to return to the battlefield and slaughter the enemy in the name of vengeance.

My mother said that this was among her favorite poems of all time—which is why I memorized it and did such a good job reciting it to my fourth grade class that when I finished, everybody just sat there in creeped-out silence, until Mrs. Haber told me, in a tone that indicated I'd done something wrong, "That was a very unusual choice, Bobby. Now please take your seat."

7

Speak, Memory

Barry Gardner and I were looking out his living room window, admiring the Coney Island parachute jump, looming like the Eiffel Tower on the other side of Brooklyn, when we heard the news that Pope John XXIII had died.

That guy's been pope forever, I thought, as I turned towards the TV. Just then Barry's mother, Priscilla, walked past the television, on her way to the kitchen, but didn't stop to listen more carefully—apparently because she didn't care about a dead pope, and neither did anybody else in this house of Jews (who'd changed their name from Goldberg). Nobody said a word about it.

The afternoon of Monday, June 3, 1963, passed like so many other Flatbush afternoons, with after-school games of chess, Clue, and Monopoly, the ordinary events of another late-spring day stretching into an evening that I most likely spent at home, with my mother and my one-year-old brother, Jerrold, but that I don't remember because it was nearly identical to every other evening of my life in 1963... and probably 1964, too. Yet that one moment in Barry's living room remains frozen in time alongside a hundred others that I now remember because somewhere a radio or TV was playing, and as the perpetual flow of information washed over me, it sometimes turned seemingly insignificant moments into scenes so vivid, I can see them with the clarity of instant replay.

Some of that information, especially the program-interrupting special bulletins about manned space shots, captivated me so completely, the world seemed to stop spinning as I listened—such as the morning of May 5, 1961, when half of PS 249, grades three through six, were lined up in the gymnasium. It was about 10:15, and we were preparing to march into the auditorium for Friday assembly, the boys in their white shirts and ties, the girls in their white blouses. I was in the third grade, and my teacher, Mrs. Feinstein, was standing in front of the assemblage, telling us to quiet down. Beside her, on a metal folding chair, was an enormous transistor radio, a "boom box," which she'd just turned on for this momentous day in American history.

An astronaut, Navy Commander Alan B. Shepard, was sitting atop a Redstone rocket in his Mercury space capsule, Freedom 7, the announcer said, and was about to be the first American launched into outer space. No, he wasn't going to orbit the earth, at 17,500 miles per hour, as Russian cosmonaut Yuri Gagarin, the first man in space (a Communist!), had done less than a month earlier—thus asserting the technical superiority of our arch-enemy, the Soviet Union, and making an entire freedom-loving nation feel distinctly inferior, both intellectually and militarily. Shepard was going to ride this rocket a mere 115 miles into space, on a 15-minute, 300-mile sub-orbital flight, at 4,500 miles per hour.

But the moment was still exciting, and tense. America, down

but not out, had picked itself up off the canvas and was fighting back, and we were experiencing it communally, as a school. Many of us were thinking the same thing: *What if the rocket blows up?* We knew such things had happened many times, though never with a man on board. But the voice on the radio was saying that everything was "A-OK" and the launch would occur in "T-minus three minutes and counting."

The gym was abuzz with nervous energy.

"Be quiet or I'll turn it off," Mrs. Feinstein threatened, above the din.

We piped down and listened in silence to the final 10 seconds of the countdown. I couldn't believe that it was really going to happen after so many missions had been "scrubbed" and "aborted" after hours-long "holds" due to bad weather and myriad technical problems. I'd wanted to witness something like this my entire life, all eight years of it. My heart was in my throat.

"Roger, liftoff, and the clock is started," said a voice on the radio.

A murmur, not quite a cheer, filled the gym as the rocket inched off the launch pad and was soon streaking towards outer space. Then it was completely quiet as we listened to the chatter coming over the radio, back and forth, between astronaut and ground control at Cape Canaveral, unfamiliar phrases, flowing like the poetry of a New Age, free verse for the Free World—and much of it would soon embed itself in the American vernacular:

Fuel is go
Oxygen is go
All systems go
One point two G

Manual yaw
What a beautiful view!

And then the ride back down:

Start retro sequence
Periscope retracted and going into re-entry attitude
Trajectory right on the button
Cap com, can you read now?
Freedom 7 reports good drogue
Everything A-O.K
Astronaut now on board!

Even the teachers were applauding as all the students let loose with a window-rattling roar. We'd done it, my country had done it... we'd shot a man into outer space, gotten him back alive, and it was a triumph of the American will, a counterpunch to the Communists, the first in a series of rapid-fire body blows that would ultimately bring the Soviets to their knees. The race to put a man on the moon (led by ex-Nazi scientist Wernher von Braun, a fact generally not discussed in polite company, especially by Jews) was *on*, and I couldn't imagine anything more thrilling—more thrilling than hunting Nazis, even. *Take that, Russians! That's what you get for sending that Sputnik dog into space and letting him suffocate to death 'cause you didn't know how to bring him back! You've had it coming for years!*

I was holding back tears as we all marched in lockstep into the auditorium for assembly, proud American kids in America, in 1961, ready to proudly pledge allegiance to the flag of the United States of America and to the republic for which it stands, and proudly sing the "Star-Spangled Banner" followed by

Bobby in Naziland

"This Is My Country" ("grandest on earth"), thereby achieving the required patriotic high, which would linger through the following February.

That's when I feigned a stomachache so I could stay home from school and for the first time watch live on TV as a man, Colonel John Glenn, was launched into outer space. And I saw as Glenn, in his Friendship 7 space capsule, mounted atop a powerful Atlas rocket (rather than the more reliable Redstone), "hit that keyhole in the sky" (as *Life* magazine would poetically put it), and, nearly a year after the Soviets had done it, and after Glenn's mission had already been scrubbed 10 times, became the first American to orbit the earth.

But right after the mission began, it looked as if it might turn into a horror show, the kind of catastrophe everybody knew had to happen sooner or later... though not this soon. Telemetry signals indicated that the capsule's heat shield had come loose, and if the signals were correct, then the shield would fall off, and Glenn would burn up on the way down, as temperatures outside the capsule reached 2,000 degrees Fahrenheit.

This was, more or less, what the world knew. The "experts" on TV were able to interpret the limited information mission control had made available and explain to viewers what might be going on. But ground control didn't tell Glenn, since they weren't certain and, even if they had been, there was nothing they could do about it. They wanted Glenn to concentrate on his mission without any life-threatening distractions.

Now I really was feeling sick. I hadn't cut school to see an astronaut get cremated. That kind of thing could set back Project Mercury for years. I might be in sixth grade before America tried to launch a man into space again. That was too long; the Russians would get too far ahead. They didn't care if one of their cosmonauts died. They just wouldn't tell anybody. Moscow only spoke of successful missions... when they were over and everybody was alive and safe. At least that's what I'd heard people talking about—failed missions and dead cosmonauts, lots of them.

Finally, when he'd completed his three spins around the earth and it was time for Glenn to come home, mission control alerted him that there might be a problem, though they still didn't tell him what the problem was. They only said: *Don't jettison your retro rockets after firing them. Leave them strapped to the heat shield.* This, they hoped, might hold the shield in place just long enough to give Glenn a fighting chance.

I could barely stand the three horrible minutes of radio silence that mission control had announced would occur during reentry. I stared at a diagram on the TV of the ionic forces engulfing Glenn's capsule, disrupting communications.

"We should be hearing something any moment now," the commentator said, practically under his breath.

Then I (and the rest of the Free World) heard Glenn's voice crackling loud and clear: "Hello, Cape. Friendship 7. Do you receive? Over." Astronaut and capsule were A-O.K., and the men of mission control (they were all men) stood up and cheered—it was faulty telemetry, not a faulty heat shield.

I leapt off the couch, feeling a rush of pure joy for another great American feat of daring and skill.

"You've recovered quickly," my mother noted.

"Yes," I said. "I'm feeling much better."

That night, I inducted Marine Colonel John H. Glenn, Jr. into my personal pantheon of American heroes, right next to Roger Maris, who, I thought, looked as good in Yankee pinstripes as Glenn did in a silver space suit. But while Maris let his bat

Bobby in Naziland

do his talking—never, as far as I know, saying a memorable word—Glenn had captured my imagination with his quip about the molten bits of disintegrating retro rocket flying past Friendship 7's window like a meteor shower: "Boy, that was a real fireball!"

Mostly, though, what I heard on the TV and radio were bland voices uttering hourly the names of assorted dictators and bureaucratic functionaries, names that ceased to be names and instead became meaningless sounds, poetic in their own way, drilled into my brain by rote repetition: Andrei Gromyko... U Thant... Sukarno... Gamal Abdel Nasser... Nguyễn Cao Kỳ... Madame Nhu...

A half-century later, these names have become the improbable sounds of nostalgia. Somebody on TV mentions Madame Nhu, for example, and it fills my head not with newsreel images of South Vietnam, but with pictures of Flatbush as it used to be—a neighborhood that I now realize must have looked like the Promised Land to the survivors and refugees who'd fled the Third Reich. Flatbush was a place without gas chambers or crematoria, where death was a natural occurrence and mass murder unheard of. Even for me, the dreary landscape of my youth becomes a wistful wonderland when I conjure it on my computer with a single mouse-click. It's all there: the antique photos of East 17th Street itself; the videos of decades-ago-cancelled TV shows that I once watched every day after school, like *Terrytoons Circus*, with its grotesque clown selling Snickers bars to children; the advertisements for toys I once owned, like Ideal's Fireboat with its water-squirting cannons, or coveted, like Remco's Whirlybird, "the biggest, most spectacular helicopter ever made." And each one is another piece of a lost world, creating a confluence of organic memory and digital archive so intertwined, sometimes I can't tell where biology ends and electronics begin.

Then there are those fragments of memory that couldn't possibly exist, yet something memory-like lingers—a tiny quivering in the recesses of my brain, or the dim echoes of a sound and the ghost of an image... like the day when I was six months old and my parents took me to a zoo, on Long Island, where a spider monkey reached out of its cage, grabbed my index finger and started gnawing on it like a drum stick, chewing it down to the bone, and letting go only when my father pounded frantically on the cage. Yet when I look at the scar, which never faded, it seems as if I can almost see the monkey with my finger in its mouth and hear myself shrieking and my parents screaming bloody murder—maybe because I've heard that story so many times.

But they never told me about the events of November 1, 1952, the day that, on Eniwetok Atoll, a small spit of coral in the middle of the Pacific Ocean, America detonated the first hydrogen bomb, a nuclear weapon 750 times more powerful than the atomic bomb that had incinerated Hiroshima, seven years earlier.

I was 97 days old when a one-footed Jewish refugee from Nazi Germany, Edward Teller, the *real* Dr. Strangelove, more commonly known as "the father of the H-bomb," introduced Planet Earth to this brand-new way to exterminate the human race. So I don't know what I sensed when "Mike," as the bomb was quaintly code-named, tore asunder the very fabric of reality. But I must have sensed something—the sound of the explosion on the radio, perhaps, or an infinitesimal, almost imperceptible, increase in tension the next time my mother touched me. Because there's no way that that primal blast, which vaporized the test site, didn't penetrate the consciousness of my parents, who must have at least taken pause at the idea that they'd brought me into the world just in time to greet the hydrogen bomb.

Or maybe not. Maybe they were too preoccupied with the screaming bundle of joy in the bassinette at the foot of their bed to contemplate the abstract notion of thermonuclear annihilation. As cataclysmic as the H-bomb might have been, it wasn't all that different from the atomic bomb, which I know they liked very much because, as my mother often said, "If it weren't for the atom bomb, your father would have had to invade Japan, and he might not be here today." Meaning neither would I. So, if anything, my parents, who were practical people and not in the habit of metaphysical speculation, probably absorbed this bit of news and got on with the business of feeding another mouth.

With me, however, perhaps some lingering consciousness of that first H-bomb contributed, beginning in late 1962, to my prolonged phase of obsessively drawing pictures of mushroom clouds—one of my more successful efforts being a chaotic red and orange crayon illustration which seemed to viscerally capture the bomb's destructive force and which graced the cover of my science report "Our Friend the Atom." But I strongly suspect that the primary inspiration behind my Mushroom-Cloud Period was my certainty during the Cuban Missile Crisis, in October of that year, that nuclear war was imminent and that, like Eniwetok Atoll, I, too, would be vaporized.

I spent an entire week wondering if vaporization was going to hurt or if it was going to happen so fast I'd never know what hit me. One morning, I sat in Mrs. Ortiz's fifth grade class watching her write the lyrics to "Mañana" on the blackboard—in an effort to teach us a word of Spanish while instilling the accepted notion that all Mexicans were inherently lazy. As I looked around at my classmates lustily singing "*Mañana* is soon enough for me..." I thought: How can anybody pretend this is an ordinary day? And why are we singing about *mañana* when we might all be dead tomorrow? I knew that when the air raid sirens sounded, duck-and-cover wasn't going to save anybody from the H-bomb. I'd known that since the first grade, when we were introduced to duck-and-cover drills, and even then, as we all crouched under our wooden desks, it was cause for silly jokes—*I hope a bomb doesn't fall on my back*—and surreptitious laughter, an early lesson in officially sanctioned absurdity.

I was 10 years old. I didn't want to die.

8

Midsummer 1952

She always began with the heat wave that baked New York City that July. "It was 95 degrees every day," she'd say. "Some days it hit a hundred. And we didn't even have an air conditioner. Do you have any idea how uncomfortable it was to be nine months pregnant in that miserable little apartment?"

It so happens I had a very good idea of how it felt to endure sweltering summers in an un-air-conditioned apartment—because we still lived in one. But since my mother's question was about being pregnant and hot rather than just being hot, I'd say nothing and wait for her to make the inevitable transition to the next part of her tale, the part that, like the capture of Adolf Eichmann, bore a Buenos Aires dateline: On the night of July 26, 12 hours before I was born, Eva Perón—"Evita"—the first lady of Argentina, died, at age 33, of cervical cancer.

"It was on the front page of all the newspapers the day you were born," she'd say, though by this point I wasn't listening—because Evita had nothing to do with me or anything I cared about.

But now, every time I hear Eva Perón's name, I picture my

mother in that apartment, in her sweat-drenched maternity clothes, sitting on the couch in front of a sputtering old floor fan, *The New York Times* resting on her bulging belly, as the dual drama of the imminent birth of her first child and the terminal illness of a young Argentinian celebrity, the Princess Di of her day, enthralls her.

It was Perón's rise from obscurity to become a savior of the poor and downtrodden, "The Lady of Hope," as she was known, that so mesmerized my mother. "She was dirt poor," she'd say, as if she were talking about one of our neighbors, like Mary Coogan on the first floor. "She came from *nothing*." My mother believed that anybody with enough brains and ambition could transcend poverty and obscurity and become *somebody*—even the first lady of a major South American country. Or at least she hoped that was the case.

Or maybe she just had a thing for iconic foreign politicians, like Winston Churchill, of whom she said, "I liked him more than Roosevelt. He was the one I listened to on the radio during the worst days of the war, when we thought we were going to lose."

But I didn't want to hear about Churchill, either, or Roosevelt, or any other politician, for that matter. Because, with the notable exceptions of myself, after being elected third-grade class president the same year I played the First Amendment in a school play about the Bill of Rights (typecasting, I presume— every day at three o'clock I'd run into the schoolyard crying, "Freedom!"), and Abraham Lincoln, because of the soaring language of his Gettysburg Address, which I'd been memorizing for pleasure, I thought *all* politicians were boring, and I didn't care what country they came from.

There was another story about that summer that I would have liked to hear, but my mother never told it to me, probably because she was too caught up in Evita and her new baby to notice. I found out about it 57 years later, when I was reading Perón's obituary in the microfilm files at the New York Public Library. It, too, was featured on the front page: At midnight, on July 26 — nine hours before I came into the world, bearing a headful of blond curls (as I was often told) — a pilot and a stewardess on a National Airlines flight approaching Washington, D.C., saw a series of "strange objects" flying above their plane. A sergeant on the ground, at Andrews Air Force Base, saw them, too, as did about a thousand other people, including members of President Truman's staff. Radar confirmed it: Objects unknown, traveling at speeds between 100 and 7,000 miles per hour, were buzzing Washington. There's even movie footage of these UFOs — a dozen specks of light streaking behind the Capitol dome.

It happened again on the night of July 27, when I was 12 hours old. The pilot of a Capital Airlines flight taking off from Washington National reported seeing 11 "odd lights," and the Air Force sent up a plane to investigate. The "saucers," as *The New York Times* and other major newspapers called these unidentified objects, then outran the jet, leaving it in their cosmic dust. And that was that. But, I've wondered since my discovery, does it *mean* anything that I was born on the day that the rash of UFO sightings of 1952 had reached a frenzied apogee just as the first lady of Argentina was passing into the great beyond? Had the aliens come for me *and* Evita? *Was it all connected?*

Judging by everything else the *Times* found fit to print that Sunday morning, I'd say probably not. Despite UFOs, Evita, and the heat, life appeared to be proceeding normally in seemingly quaint little old New York City, where telephone numbers still began with prefixes like INgersoll, NIghtingale, and BUckingham; women engaged to be married were called "affianced"; and, according to advertisements, you could buy a summer dress for 11 bucks, a men's tropical wool suit for $44.75, an English racing bike for $38.98, a round-trip ticket on Eastern Airlines from New York to Havana for $187, and a house in Forest Hills for $13,650—or you could rent a 3½-room apartment on Sutton Place for $209 a month. (Though as the help-wanted ads made clear, the going salary for an entry-level white-collar job was about 50 bucks a week—which may partially explain why my father went into the candy store business.)

Clues to the nature of life elsewhere on the planet could be found in other parts of the paper: A full-page ad for "healthy" cigarettes declared, "More Doctors Smoke Camels"... The stock market was at a 22-year high after a week of moderate gains... King Farouk of Egypt had been deposed in a bloodless coup... A woman flying Pan American airlines, from Rio de Janeiro to Rome, was sucked out of the plane off the coast of Brazil when the emergency door popped open... The Korean War raged on, as B-29s pounded North Korea's electrical power grid... *The Caine Mutiny*, by Herman Wouk, was the #1 work of fiction... *Witness*, by Whittaker Chambers, was the #1 work of nonfiction...

And over in the sports section, a universe unto itself, the Summer Olympic Games were ongoing in Helsinki, where Bob Mathias, an American, had broken his own world record for the decathlon... The New York Yankees were in first place in the American League... The Brooklyn Dodgers were in first place in the National League... Stan Musial, of the St. Louis Cardinals, batting .325, was leading the National League... Billy Goodman, of the Boston Red Sox, batting .330, was leading the American League... and Cleveland Indians third baseman Al Rosen, the second in a very short line of "Hebrew Hammers" (and the best Jewish slugger since the original Hebrew Hammer, Hank

Bobby in Naziland

Greenberg), was leading the A.L. with 18 home runs, 4 more than Mickey Mantle of the Yankees.

How comforting it felt that day in the library to look upon this mid-century snapshot of reality, of an American empire approaching its zenith—it was as if I'd returned to the days when I carried in my head dozens of phone numbers that began with those mysterious prefixes, and when I was surrounded by people who spoke daily and passionately of Mantle, Musial, and Mathias. Indeed, to look upon Mickey Mantle's name in the box score of a game against the Detroit Tigers, played more than 50 years ago—he homered and knocked in four runs, but the Yanks still lost, 10-6—filled me with the hallucinatory sense that everything at that time was just as it should be. Yet, this *New York Times* reality might as well have been fiction, it bore so little resemblance to my personal reality, the one I faced every day—the one that consisted of a third-floor walkup in a second-rate apartment building, the teeming street in front of the building, and the inexorable existence around the corner, on Church Avenue, a mere 174 steps (I counted) from my front door, of the family albatross, otherwise known as my father's candy store.

9

The Great Candy-Store Tragedy

Forget about Nazis and death camps. If you want to know what really haunted us, let's talk about the candy store. To hear my mother tell it, you'd think the candy store was a worse tragedy than the Holocaust—because not a day passed when she didn't have to endure the shame of being married to a soda jerk. She didn't care that the store, which was little more than a hole in the wall next to the subway station, had been paying her bills since 1948—she despised the place and everything it stood for, and she taught me and my father to despise it, too... not that my father needed any help.

All we wanted was for someone to come along and take the damn candy store off our hands. And we waited for this mythical buyer as if we were waiting for Godot. But my uncle Herb, my father's younger brother, thought that arson might be a better idea, and he wrote a song about it, kind of a lullaby, really, which he crooned to me every time I saw him. I usually sang along:

Take a can of kerosene
Put it by the door

Bobby in Naziland

Take a match
Give a scratch
No more candy store...

The Duke Snider story, however, seemed to contradict everything I'd ever heard about the store, and strangely enough, it was my mother who liked to tell it, because, next to Jackie Robinson, Snider was her favorite Dodger, and she happened to be in the store—six months pregnant with me—the afternoon, early in the 1952 season, that he walked in and said to my father, who was behind the counter, "I hear you got the best egg creams on Church Avenue."

"Specialty of the house," my father said, proceeding to whip up one of his chocolate masterpieces. But he must have found it galling to wait on Snider, because deep down he probably thought that if a couple of breaks had gone the other way, *he* could have been the famous athlete—a star running back on the New York football Giants, maybe—dropping down from Valhalla every so often to order an egg cream from the schnook on Church Avenue.

Snider, who was living a block away, on East 18th Street, on the "good side" of Church Avenue, laid a dime on the counter, drank the egg cream, thanked my father, and walked into the subway station next door to take the Brighton Express one stop to Ebbets Field for his game against the Boston Braves.

That was the whole story, and yes, it lacked certain crucial details that I'd have liked to hear—like *who* told Snider that my father had the best egg creams on Church Avenue? One of his neighbors, perhaps? Or had another Dodger, like Gil Hodges, who also lived in the neighborhood, walked into the store and, incognito, sampled an egg cream? Did the Dodgers talk about my father's egg creams in the locker room? And if they were so good, how come Snider never came back for another one? Did he find a better egg cream at a different candy store on another street? Or did he just move to Bay Ridge soon afterwards?

Nobody knew. Still, every time I heard that story—and this is one that I *asked* my mother to tell—it sounded like a fairy tale. It didn't seem possible that a major league baseball player, a center fielder who'd hit 407 home runs over the course of his career and would wind up in Cooperstown, no less, had ever set foot in my father's candy store.

But the story was true. And I think Snider's visitation goes a long way towards explaining my father's perverse hatred of the Brooklyn Dodgers and his love of the rival New York Giants. No team had caused the Dodgers as much misery as the Giants, and no more so than on the afternoon of October 3, 1951, in the Polo Grounds, in the bottom of the ninth inning of the playoff game that people would continue to talk about decades after it had happened and both teams had long ago deserted New York for California. That was the day that Giants outfielder and third baseman Bobby Thomson came to bat against Ralph Branca, with one out, runners on second and third, and the Giants, who'd come from 13½ games back to force the playoff series, trailing 4-2.

It was the primal sports myth that I was raised on, that was infused into my soul, the most exciting thing that had ever happened in New York City, something so amazing, nothing like it could ever happen again. Chesterfield Cigarettes, who'd sponsored the Giants broadcasts, had given my father (who sold plenty of Chesterfields) a promotional 78 rpm recording of announcer Russ Hodges's play-by-play of Thomson's at-bat— the most famous call in the history of baseball, captured only by some guy in Brooklyn who was listening to the game on the radio and decided to turn on his tape recorder. The record was cracked but still playable, and I played it all the time. Though my mother had taught me to hate the Giants, I loved the sound of ecstasy in Hodges's voice, scratchy from too many cigarettes, as he cries, at the crack of the bat, "There's a long drive... it's gonna be, I believe... *The Giants win the pennant! The Giants win the pennant!... The Giants win the pennant and they're going crazy! I don't believe it.... I do not believe it!*"

Thomson's three-run "shot heard 'round the world"—the Miracle of Coogan's Bluff (the place in uptown Manhattan where the Polo Grounds were located)—had propelled the Giants into the all–New York World Series against the Yankees and sent every Dodgers fan in Brooklyn and beyond into a tearful state of deep and prolonged shock and despair.

If my father let on that any of this was going through his head as he served that egg cream to The Duke of Flatbush, who'd witnessed Thomson's home run from his position in center field, he never said.

So virulent was my father's hatred of the candy store, in his later years he refused to talk about it, acting as if the store had never existed, as if having owned it were a war crime or, worse, a humiliating personal failure that had dragged down his entire family.

The humiliation, I think, was the result of its having taken him 17 years of unceasing effort to finally sell the store. And this was exacerbated by the fact that, in 1963, he thought he *had* sold it. But the buyer refused to pay off the "note," and my father had to repossess the store after believing for a month that he was free at last from his albatross. Then he had to return to those grueling 12-hour shifts, the ones that began in the predawn

Church Avenue gloom, when the drunks came staggering out of Byrne's "gin mill" across the street and made their way to the candy store's front window to croak, "Bromo Seltzer." And my father would serve it to them, one foaming glassful of stomach-settling swill after another, 12 cents a pop, thereby earning his first dollar of the day.

That was his life for 17 years: Two weeks of working all day in the store, then coming home in the evening to eat, argue with my mother, go to sleep, and wake up at 3:45 a.m. to walk around the corner and do it again—until it was time to switch to the night shift for the next two weeks.

I used to beg my father: "Dad, please take a vacation." But he always said he couldn't, and my mother always said that the store *had* to stay open 24 hours a day, seven days a week, or we wouldn't have enough money.

"How much is enough?" I'd ask her, but she wouldn't tell me. All she'd ever say about money was that it was to be used *only* for necessities, and that if she weren't so good at pinching pennies then we wouldn't have "what to eat." And every time I dared to ask how much money my father made, she'd spit out the same three questions: "Is there a roof over your head? Is there food on the table? Are there clothes on your back?"

Yes, I'd answer sullenly, knowing that she was going to again remind me that I should be grateful for what I had because there were children starving in Europe *and* China.

But I wasn't grateful; I was money-crazy. I wanted money. I loved the look and the feel and the smell of it. I once had 15 dollars—5- and 10-dollar bills—that I kept in a glass jar on the dresser in my bedroom. Sometimes I'd take the money out of the jar, hold it in front of my face, and just stare at it. One night my uncle Paul, my mother's younger brother, walked in and saw me

Bobby in Naziland

lying in bed, entranced by Alexander Hamilton's picture on the 10-dollar bill.

"Look at this kid," he called to my mother, in the kitchen. "He's lying there staring at money. If he's not a millionaire by the time he's 30, he's going to kill himself."

My mother was probably too embarrassed to tell me that my father made what I now suspect was about 85 bucks a week. However, if I sat quietly in my room, especially when she was in the kitchen talking to Anita Horowitz or one of her other Mahjong buddies, I'd hear a lot of things about the candy store that I wasn't supposed to—like how one night my father and a bunch of the candy store regulars, including Anita's husband, Steve, were arrested for watching "stag films" at a bachelor party my father had thrown in the store, and that my uncle Herb, the one who'd written the arson song, had to bail them all out at the police station.

One morning I awoke to the sound of my mother making one panicked phone call after another, because, as I eventually figured out, her father, Isidor, the candy store's co-owner, had been arrested *again*, and my father had to bail him out at the Tombs. Some 45 years later, my mother finally got around to telling me that Isidor was a major bookmaker, and the candy store was his base of operations.

This was shocking—nothing I knew about my grandfather, who seemed to possess only the vaguest outlines of a personality, indicated that he'd had a taste for vice. Actually, all I knew about him were the most basic facts of his life, which I'd learned from other people: born in Germany, came to New York, fought in World War I, and managed a chain of supermarkets during the Depression, a job that my mother had said paid him $75 a week—a fortune at the time. She'd also mentioned that "Poppy," as I called him, had dropped out of rabbinical school—though she never said why. And neither did Poppy. Because he wasn't a talker. He was so quiet, the only time you'd know he was around was when he was sleeping. Then he snored like a buzz saw. And when he was awake, my grandmother Helen was always telling him what she didn't like about him: the food he ate, the clothes he wore, the scent of his after-shave lotion, his collection of Jerry Vale albums.

"Why are you always buying records, Isidor?" she'd ask. "They're a waste of money and we already have enough crap in this house."

My grandfather would pretend she wasn't there.

"Isidor, you're a sheep," she'd say. "You *never* stand up for yourself."

As I now realize, my grandmother must have known about my grandfather's girlfriends—another one of Poppy's secrets that I found out about only after he'd been dead for 30 years. My brother told me about it the same day he told me that our uncle Paul was crashing on his living room couch because his wife had thrown him out of their apartment—apparently, there was something to the rumor that when she was in the Hamptons, he was home, bringing both women and men into their bed. In a rare moment of candor, Paul had told my brother, Jerrold, that, adultery-wise, he was even more indiscriminate than his father, Isidor. "The apple doesn't fall far from the tree," Paul said. Which at least shed some light on a number of childhood mysteries, like why my grandmother slept in a separate bed (next to a glass of water containing her false teeth), and perhaps why she had had a nervous breakdown, resulting in a round of electroshock therapy—which, at the time, seemed to me like just more random emotional chaos that in some way I was responsible for.

All of which is not to suggest that the candy store was little more than a den of pornography, gambling, and adultery. I'm just saying that the vice squad arrested my father and grandfather a little too often for anybody's comfort, and each time they did, it gave my mother one more reason to despise the store and its sleazy atmosphere of disrepute. And that's why both my mother and I clung to the belief that one day my father would sell the store, everything would change, and we'd live happily ever after with our $50,000. That was the magic number I always heard bandied about—the price that somebody would pay for the candy store, and it sounded like a fantastic amount of money.

When my father finally did sell the store, in 1965—to a trio of monopolistic brothers who also bought the candy store on the corner and the one across the street (thereby establishing themselves as the egg-cream kings of Church Avenue)—all he got was $28,000, which he split with Poppy. One week my father would pick up the note, $140, and the next week my grandfather would pick it up. And that's what we lived on—70 bucks a week, plus whatever was left over from the down payment.

I don't remember exactly when I began to think it was strange that my father called World War II "the best years" of his life. But at a certain point, probably when I was about 11, I did begin to wonder what he thought was so fantastic about a three-year military stint that included such inglorious lowlights as being twice "busted" back to corporal after having been promoted to sergeant, because, he said, he "didn't like taking orders"; being temporarily blinded when an artillery shell blew up in his face (Hysterial blindness? Shell shock? Nobody ever said);

and inexplicably refusing that Purple Heart he'd rightfully earned after getting hit in the ass with a piece of shrapnel—either because he thought the wound sounded vaguely absurd, or because he thought that when 1,200 of his division comrades had come home in coffins or had never come home at all, accepting a medal for a superficial injury was just wrong. And if the army was really so fucking great, then why didn't he re-enlist for four more years when the war was over and he was invited to come back as a lieutenant?

The answer to all the above mysteries was: *the candy store*. Working there year after year, with no end in sight, had made World War II look to him like, if not necessarily a good time, at least a meaningful one. Which made me further wonder: Why, in God's name, did my father, three years after the war, at age 25, get together with my grandfather Isidor, whom he never particularly liked, and buy a candy store on Church Avenue? Did he have even the slightest inkling of what he was getting into, that the very existence of the candy store would crush both his soul and my mother's soul—my mother, who believed it was her birthright to marry a respected, highly paid Jewish *professional*?

As far as my father's side of the family was concerned, owning a candy store was worse than being in jail. I heard my grandmother and uncles say stuff like that all the time—only some 30 years later did I realize that they didn't know what they were talking about. How could they not see that the candy store was romantic? Not romantic like fighting Nazis maybe, but still romantic in that inimitable atmospheric way of a Brooklyn that no longer exists.

If you read comic books, then you may remember that Pop Tate's Chock'lit Shoppe was the Riverdale institution where Archie,

Bobby in Naziland

Betty, Veronica, and Jughead whiled away idyllic afternoons sipping malteds at the gleaming, chrome-trimmed counter. It occurred to me one not-so-bad Flatbush afternoon, as I was perusing the latest editions of *Archie*, *Richie Rich*, *Sad Sack*, *Superman*, *The Flash*, *Fantastic Four*, and *Mad*, which I'd spread out on top of the ice cream freezer in the back of the store, that if Pop Tate's were in Bizarro World, the cube-shaped planet from *Superman* where everything is the opposite of the way it is on Earth, then it might look something like the Goodrose Cigar Store.

Any similarities between Tate's and Goodrose ended at the quality of the malteds—both were excellent. From that point on, Goodrose—named after my grandfather, Goodstein, and my father, Rosen—was strictly Bizarro World Tate's, beginning with my father's "literature" cronies, who, unlike the Archie gang, smoked French cigarettes while standing around deconstructing the latest "dirty" book—like *Last Exit to Brooklyn*—to appear in the special rack in the back of the store, adjacent to the phone booth, the communications hub of my grandfather's bookmaking and adultery operations. The non-similarities then progressed across every Goodrose surface, which—save for the two-foot-long Formica countertop where my father served his malteds and egg creams—appeared to be coated with a half-century of accumulated dust and grime. And they climaxed in the gunk-encrusted, vermin-infested corridor, behind the door with the dirty-book rack, that smelled like a dank cave filled with decomposing animals and led to a toilet that looked as if it had never been cleaned and that I'd use only in dire emergencies.

To my mother, the candy store symbolized all that was unwholesome in the world, a place that, like Dante's Inferno, was devoid of hope, a place that would have required nothing short of total demolition and reconstruction to make it look even halfway as presentable as Tate's.

Yet undeterred by the filth and the funk, the store's loyal patrons kept coming back for more egg creams, cigarettes, conversation, literature, and gambling—which is how the Goodrose generated enough cash to keep us solvent for those 17 years.

Every Sunday afternoon I watched my father stuff the weekly receipts into a canvas bag—thick wads of bills and heavy rolls of coins; it must have been a thousand dollars—and then deposit the bag in the after-hours slot at the bank on Ocean Avenue. Though a thousand dollars might have been a lot of money in the late 1950s, profit margins were razor-thin, since most of it went to pay the store's basic operating expenses, leaving barely enough take-home crumbs for my father to put food on the table. Which is probably why when I brought home a bad mark from school, my mother would inevitably ask me, her firstborn, for whom she held such high hopes, "Do you want to end up like your father, jerking sodas in a candy store?"

No, I didn't want to end up like my father, jerking sodas in a candy store, because I couldn't imagine a more shameful job... a job so shameful that sometimes when I walked by the store with my friends, I refused to acknowledge my father standing at the window—an act of disrespect I'd hear about from my mother for the next 40 years.

"You used to walk by the store and pretend your father wasn't there," she'd say, as if she had nothing to do with putting such an idea in my head.

Because my parents saw everything through the prism of the candy store, I always had to watch what I said. They accused me of being "selfish" if I expressed joy when school was closed for a snow day, because that meant that my father had to get up even earlier than usual to shovel the snow in front of the store, and spread rock salt, too, which irritated his hands. Twice his hands had been burned when a book of matches burst into flame as he was handing it to a customer with a pack of cigarettes, freak accidents my mother referred to whenever she wanted to impress upon me how difficult my father's shameful job was. To hear her tell it, you'd think he suffered the torments of Jesus on the cross—like the one hanging over each bed in the Coogans' apartment—to keep us fed, clothed, and housed.

"We're not poor," she'd tell me. "But we would be if I didn't know how to stretch a dollar."

No matter what she said, I still enjoyed working in the candy store. It gave me pleasure to organize the soda bottles in the antique cooler, a refrigerated chest filled with ice water; to rotate the candy for freshness and dust it with a feather duster; to open cartons of cigarettes and stock the individual packs in their proper slots behind the ancient steel hulk of the cash register. My father had bought the machine second-hand, in 1948, when the store opened, and while the markings on the one-cent through 10-cent keys had been obliterated from overuse, the one-dollar key, the largest denomination the register offered, was in near-pristine condition. Press the keys and the prices popped up in the register window like tiny tombstones.

Since I was the boss's son, I could also eat all the candy and ice cream I wanted to eat, drink all the soda I wanted to drink, read all the comic books I wanted to read, and collect all the baseball, football, dinosaur, Civil War, and *Mars Attacks!* cards I wanted to collect. I just wasn't allowed to say how much I liked doing these things—even though my inability to acquire the rare

Roger Maris card from the Topps '62 series this way tempered my enjoyment.

I was seven the first time my father paid me the minimum wage of one dollar an hour to sit by the window and make change for newspapers, which, before the great newspaper strike of 1962 killed off half of them, included: the *Daily News*, *The New York Times*, the *New York Post*, the *New York Herald Tribune*, the *New York World-Telegram & Sun*, the *New York Daily Mirror*, the *New York Journal-American*, and the Yiddish *Daily Forward*, as well as a full complement of the unsavory rags, like *Midnight*, with its "Where to Buy Mail Order Love Slaves" headlines, and the somewhat more upscale *National Enquirer*, which in those days trafficked primarily in gaudily illustrated front-page stories about murderers who fed their victims' bodies to vultures, and mummified corpses that people had stashed in their bedroom closets (because, like Norman Bates in *Psycho*, they couldn't let go of Mother). Children with bizarre diseases, like the one that turned 5-year-old boys into 80-year-old men, was another *Enquirer* staple, followed closely by the ever-popular thalidomide-deformed babies who had flippers instead of arms and little stubs for legs—which must have contributed to my recurring dreams of limbless children and macabre machines slicing off my own legs.

Both the *Enquirer* and *Midnight* hung on a rod above the window, out of customers' reach, and if somebody wanted to buy one of them, he or she had to ask for it by name. It never ceased to amaze me how many people asked for these tabloids as if requesting something as ordinary as a pack of Life Savers— like the old woman in the faded gray raincoat, from East 18th Street, who came around like clockwork every Wednesday, late in the afternoon, to buy an *Enquirer* and a carton of Lucky

Bobby in Naziland

Strikes. I'd take the paper off the clip and hand it to her, thrilled to have a legitimate reason to touch the ungodly thing and sneak a quick peek at whatever deformed specimen of humanity was emblazoned across the front page that week.

Yes, I, too, was dying to read the *Enquirer*—my enquiring mind wanted to know about those people who stashed their dead mothers in closets and those kids my own age who looked older than my grandfather. But the paper seemed more obscene than pornography, and I was too embarrassed to be seen reading it or even looking at it as it hung tantalizingly within my reach on the rod above the window.

The most valuable skill I learned at the candy store was how to mix the perfect egg cream. It was kind of like drawing a perfect pint of Guinness: You had to use just the right amounts of chocolate syrup and milk, and you had to squirt the seltzer against the side of the glass at just the right angle and with just the right force, so the head was neither too foamy nor not foamy enough. (A master egg-cream maker, like my father, could divert the seltzer with a spoon into a second and third glass and still achieve a perfect head.)

The reason the Goodrose Cigar Store served what some (like Duke Snider) considered the best egg creams on Church Avenue was because we used, according to my father, the best chocolate syrup money could buy, syrup that was far superior to the cheap slop they used at the competing candy stores on the corner and across the street. And the proof was in the people who lined up five-deep on hot summer days to drink our egg creams.

By late 1959 I'd developed into a good enough soda jerk to solo behind the counter and serve our legions of thirsty customers the 10-cent glasses of chocolate nectar they'd often imbibe with the traditional side, a two-cent stick pretzel. I'd watch with satisfaction as some of them returned three or four times a day to lay another dime on the semi-clean Formica counter, order another egg cream, and gasp with pure animal delight as they drained the glass in one enormous gulp.

One customer liked to order "rainbow egg creams," as he called them, a brownish-pink concoction containing a tiny squirt of every flavor of syrup we had: chocolate, vanilla, strawberry, coffee, cherry, root beer, sarsaparilla, raspberry, lemon, lime, Coca-Cola, and Tab. I thought this was such an excellent idea, I started making them for myself, not because they tasted especially good—they didn't—but because I could, for free.

I'd never heard the expression "two cents plain" before an old man walked in and ordered one.

"What?" I said.

"Seltzer," he answered, "plain seltzer."

"Well, why didn't you say so?" I said, drawing a glass from the fountain. "And it's *five* cents."

I occasionally put together the Sunday papers, too, collating on a splintered old board the various sections of the *Times* and the *Daily News* as delivery trucks dropped them off over the course of a Saturday night and Sunday morning. I did it the first time in the fall of '61, filling in for the regular newspaper guy and staying up later than I ever had in my life, in the company of my father and his cronies, who hung around all night, smoking cigarettes, drinking egg creams, and hotly debating the great question of the day: "What kind of crazy-ass name is Yelberton?"—which is what the "Y" stood for in Y. A. Tittle, the name of the quarterback the Giants had just acquired from the San Francisco 49ers. It wasn't until after midnight that somebody finally slammed the palm of his hand on the countertop and declared, to the rowdy assent of the others, "I don't give a rat's ass if his name is Y. A. Fucking Hitler... as long as the Giants win!"

Then, as everything on Church Avenue, except the bars and the candy store, started to shut down, people who couldn't wait to read the Sunday papers began to wander in to buy whatever sections were available, sometimes paying full price for just the *New York Times* classifieds or the *Daily News* comics.

I'd only half-completed the collating job when my mother came by at 2 a.m. to take me home, and my father handed me a 10-dollar bill for 10 hours' work—the most I'd ever earned in a day. As soon as I got home, I stashed it in the big Mason jar on my dresser, which already contained $11, money I told myself I was going to use to go to college so that I, the son of the best soda jerk on Church Avenue, would never have to work in a candy store when I grew up.

10

Carefully Taught

My father and his brother-in-law, my uncle Paul, the one who'd given me the fishing rod the Puerto Ricans had stolen, never missed an opportunity to rag on "welfare queens"—black women who, they said, "breed like roaches and drive around in purple Cadillacs, but don't have a pot to piss in."

It was garden-variety bigotry, inane and vicious at the same time, and it reached a fever pitch whenever the three of us were driving somewhere, usually in my uncle's silver-gray Cadillac. Every time Paul—it was always Paul—spotted a black person crossing the street, he'd say to my father, who rode shotgun, "Look! There's a nigger! Let's run him down!"

And as Paul accelerated just enough to make it seem as if he really were going to do it, he'd look at me in the rear-view mirror—I usually sat in the back—and, flashing a wicked grin, say, "You get two points for every nigger you run down."

"And three points if you run down a pregnant Puerto Rican," my father would add.

And they'd both have a good laugh.

Let's call a spade a spade: My father and uncle were hardcore,

Bobby in Naziland

old-school, "nigger-hating Jews"—and proud of it. But everyone else I knew hated black people—Jew and goyim alike. I heard this kind of shit everywhere: at home, in the candy store, in public school, in Hebrew school, at Boy Scout meetings, and in the street. More-Jewish-than-Tel-Aviv Flatbush—where (it should be noted) the police, in 1997, would arrest Abner Louima for the crime of walking while black, take him back to the 70th Precinct, and, in the name of justice, sodomize him with a broom handle—was a neighborhood rife with fomenting hatred of anything and anybody that was different. It was a neighborhood where any hint of non-conformity was aggressively non-tolerated, and *nigger*—or *schvartze*, for those who preferred the Yiddish epithet—was about as different as you could get, except for maybe *faggot*, but gay people, apparently, knew enough to keep their gayness to themselves—unless they wanted to be treated worse than "niggers."

Forget all that business about Jackie Robinson integrating Major League Baseball with the Dodgers and making it look as if Brooklyn were some kind of racially harmonious mecca. That was an aberration, the high-profile exception that proved the rule—the rule that would one day make it necessary for the Voting Rights Act, a law generally applied to the states of the former Confederacy, to be applied to Brooklyn, too. You want to know what Flatbushians thought of Jackie Robinson? *Let the nigger play. Just don't let him live on my street.* That's what they thought, and that's why he lived in the marginally more integrated environs of *East* Flatbush, the neighborhood my parents had fled in 1953—because too many black folks had been moving in, and they didn't care that one of them happened to be a Brooklyn Dodger.

The racism at Ten Mile River Boy Scout camp, where I spent

88

two weeks in the summer of 1963, was even more virulent—
it was like an endless tape loop that began at reveille. Before
they'd even crawled out of their sleeping bags, my fellow
Scouts, usually the ones from Queens and Staten Island, started
spouting "nigger jokes," and they kept it up throughout the day
with a litany of *coon*, *spade*, *jig*, *jigaboo*, *jungle bunny*, *pickaninny*,
and *spearchucker*, sometimes bursting into song with verses like
"There's a nigger in the grass/With a bullet up his ass/Take it
out! Take it out!/Like a good Boy Scout," until finally, after Taps,
the scoutmaster had to tell everybody to shut the hell up and go
to sleep already.

At Ten Mile River that summer, I learned to build a lean-
to, shoot a rifle, paddle a canoe, and tell more "nigger jokes"
than I ever knew existed. There was one joke in particular that I
heard every day, always delivered with the well-honed "ghetto"
accent that my bunkmates must have been practicing since the
day they first learned to talk: *"Lordy, Lordy, I donts wantsta die,"*
cries a "nigger" clinging to a cliff as he pleads with God for his
life. God, testing the man's faith, tells him to let go. He lets go
and plunges to his death. The punch line, invariably met with
howls of appreciative laughter: "And God said, 'Dirty nigger.'"

That I, too, thought this joke was hilarious and even told it
myself—though I couldn't match the performances of my brother
Scouts—is testament to the fact that this is what surrounded me.
It never occurred to me that there was another way to be. Just
as "You've Got to Be Carefully Taught" said—the song from the
South Pacific original-cast album that (all too ironically) played
over and over on the phonograph in my own house, adding the
words and music of *Jewish* Richard Rodgers and half-*Jewish*
Oscar Hammerstein to the ever-lingering mass hallucination of
World War II—you had to learn to hate everybody your relatives

Bobby in Naziland

hated while you were still a child, no older than eight.

And, boy, was I ever indoctrinated—by virtually everybody I came in contact with but especially my father, who veritably oozed hatred for any human being with a dark complexion (did he think the song was an instruction manual for child rearing, an addendum containing answers not to be found in Benjamin Spock's bible, *Baby and Child Care?*), and Paul, who was more like an older brother than an uncle and who was even more bitter than my father was, though he had far less reason to be.

Paul made a lot of money selling women's clothing, and he spent it as fast as he made it—on bespoke suits, scuba gear, that new Cadillac, a used MG, and jet-setting trips to the Caribbean, Miami Beach, Europe, and Las Vegas, as if he were an honorary member of the Rat Pack. Naturally, I idolized him, and begged him to take me with him *anywhere*, even to watch him bowl at the alley above Deal Town, across the street from the candy store, which he'd do on occasion. I found this especially entertaining because when the man appeared at the back of the lane to clear the scattered pins, I'd tell Paul to fling the ball at him. He'd actually do this sometimes, with the aim and power of a skilled athlete, sending the guy scrambling, practically diving, to get out of the way as the ball zinged past him.

Even more thrilling was when Paul took me to Coney Island to play skeeball, shoot air rifles, and go on the rides. His favorite was the Cyclone, a rickety roller coaster left over from the Roaring Twenties. At first I was too small to go on the Cyclone and would just stand there watching as my uncle, always in the first car—the scariest place to be—rode it three or four times in a row. All I wanted was to be big enough to take that lunatic ride with him. This finally happened when I was 10 and had grown, in the short time since my last trip to Coney Island, the additional fraction of an inch necessary to meet the height requirement. But my joy turned to terror as the cars made the initial stomach-churning plunge from the highest point, 80 feet up. I thought that the metal bar pressing against my lap wouldn't hold me in place, that the G-forces would send me flying out of the car and I'd fall to my death, my body splattered on the sidewalk. I held on to the bar with all my strength, and when the ride ended, I walked unsteadily away, glad to be alive. I vowed to never again set foot on the Cyclone and instead stick to the Wild Mouse and bumper cars, which were about all the thrill I could take—but I didn't tell my uncle that.

Every time Paul saw me, it was the same crazy thing: He'd walk into the house, say, "Hi, Bubblehead," wrestle me to the ground, get on top of me, lick my eyelids—he called it giving me an "eyewash"—and then tell me as he stroked my face that I had "beautiful, soft skin." He'd also pay me 25 cents an hour to massage his back like I was his personal geisha boy. And he'd take me with him to the Turkish baths, also at Coney Island, so we could sit naked in the steam room. We did nothing untoward that I can recall, but from the time I was three he called me "fag," "fagbait," and "fruit," as if these were terms of endearment. I'd be sitting in my Mickey Mouse Club chair, watching *The Mickey Mouse Club* on TV. And as the Mouseketeers sang "M-I-C-K-E-Y!" Paul would burst into the living room and sing, *"F-R-U-I-T... Mickey Fruit!"*

Yet, despite this constant barrage of teasing and torment, I continued to worship Paul, because when he returned from Germany after he got out of the army, he brought me a reversible jacket that had an embroidered map of Germany on the back of the blue suede side (which didn't seem to bother my father) and an embroidered screaming eagle on the back of the white satin

Bobby in Naziland

side. It was the coolest, most expensive piece of clothing I owned, and on the rare occasions my mother, forever worried I'd get into a fight and tear it, let me wear the jacket to school, it was as if I were clad in Joseph's Coat of Many Colors; everybody would gather around me because they wanted to touch it—nobody had ever seen a jacket like that before.

Paul also gave me hope that there was a way out of Brooklyn—even though he hadn't found his own way out. In 1963, at 24, my uncle was still living with my grandparents, in a four-room walk-up in Gravesend. He said he only slept there because it was convenient. And I believed him, because the rest of the time he lived in the alternate universe that I dreamed about living in—the one that consisted of hot cars, exotic travel, and big money. That's why I did everything I could think of to connect with Paul, to draw him into meaningful conversations. I'd ask him stuff like "What does the ocean look like from an airplane, Uncle Paul?" and "How many suede coats did you sell this month?" and "When can I meet your new girlfriend?" (It never occurred to me that he might also have boyfriends.)

I must have seemed like a stray dog, the way I sucked up to him. But I thought that if I could get him to like me enough, he'd take me with him somewhere on a jet plane, somewhere far better than Coney Island or the bowling alley, preferably to the Caribbean—I had my eye on Aruba. But I couldn't really connect with him no matter what I did, because I couldn't figure out who the fuck Paul was. How could I possibly have known that he had a secret "gay" life that he kept hidden not just from me, but from the entire family, and all he let me see was a bizarre distortion of that life? I was too young to realize that it wasn't normal for a "swinging bachelor" making $500 a week—more than my father made in a month—to live with his parents, subjecting himself to my grandmother's screaming every time he came home late and to her relentless demands to "Clean up your room!" as if he were 14. Now I wonder: Didn't one of his multitude of girlfriends and/or boyfriends ever say, "Let's go back to *your* place for a change"?

When Paul told me that his company was transferring him upstate, to Syracuse, I couldn't imagine him living on his own— he seemed totally dependent on my grandmother to keep all practical aspects of his life in proper working order, especially his laundry. And I couldn't believe that the time had finally come when I'd no longer be able to visit my grandmother and dig Paul's dirty magazines out of his closet the moment I was left alone in the house. I cherished his collection of *Playboy*s as much for the nude pictures as for the "Little Annie Fanny" cartoon strips that featured what I thought were hilarious storylines, like the "Greenback Busters" football team gang-banging Annie on their 50-yard line before a cheering, sell-out crowd. (I didn't fully grasp what was happening, but Annie's expression of wide-eyed delight as the team piled on top of her made me laugh.) Even better, though, was Paul's stash of obscure porn titles, which he must have bought on 42nd Street, and which, unlike *Playboy*, displayed great bushes of female pubic hair. It was the kind of stuff that drove me half-insane with prepubescent lust and made me think that I was going miss those magazines more than I'd miss my uncle.

Meanwhile, back at the candy store, my father was busy nurturing his well-diversified portfolio of the ethnic groups he hated, which naturally included Puerto Ricans, like the ones who stole my fishing pole, and whom he loathed because they, too, he said, were all on welfare. And though he didn't call them "spics,"

Bobby in Naziland

as many did, he often delighted his customers with a perfectly accented impression of a Puerto Rican talking Spanglish on the telephone: "*Mira! Mira!* Come to America. Get free money!"

Nor did he call the Irish "micks," but he hated them, too, because he thought they were all drunks, thugs, and cops on the take—except for Jimmy O'Sullivan, the housepainter who lived upstairs from us and was a good customer at the store. It certainly didn't improve my father's opinion when, as he told it, three Irish gangsters walked into the store one morning and tried to shake him down for protection money—then thought better of the idea when he grabbed a metal paperweight and said, "The first one who comes near me gets this in the face."

He never used the term "Polacks," either, a slur I took to mean goyim of Polish descent. Yet a small paperback book titled *It's Fun to Be a Polak!* appeared on the candy store's display rack one day and began selling briskly. Written by one Ed Zewbskewiecz, it said in the preface, "Few of our people will take offense at this book. Few of our people can read." Many times did I myself read the book from cover to cover.

As for Italians, my father didn't call them "wops" or "guineas" and even respected them because they were all, he said, "Mafioso" who, unlike Irish gangsters, knew what they were doing, but he also hated them—because they were all Mafioso and knew what they were doing.

In short, my father had it in for goyim of every stripe, but nobody more so than southern "rednecks," a variety rarely found in Flatbush, but whom he'd frequently encountered when he was in the army. "Rednecks," he explained, "hate Jews even more than they hate niggers, 'cause they think the Jews have all the money."

The way he saw it, he'd fought the Nazis for the inalienable

94

right to hate anybody he fucking wanted to hate, and this was one hard-earned privilege he was going to exercise to its fullest—along with his Second Amendment rights.

My father joined the National Rifle Association in 1964, in the aftermath of the Harlem riots—because, after watching on TV as "the niggers" torched entire city blocks, he thought that at any moment this heavily armed mob of black savages was going to overrun Flatbush, break down his door, ransack the apartment, carry off his valuables along with my mother, and then run around the corner, loot the candy store, and, for good measure, burn it to the ground to "teach whitey a lesson," as he liked to say. The NRA seemed to agree that this was indeed a likely possibility, saying as much in their monthly magazine, *American Rifleman*, in coded language that those attuned to the special frequency might interpret as: *It takes a good white man with a gun to stop a bad nigger with a gun.*

Soon enough, my father and Paul, who'd also joined the organization (which most people considered sane and "respectable"), began discussing the possibility of buying guns to "shoot some niggers," just in case the police weren't up to the job.

I, for one, didn't think they were kidding. They were both army veterans trained in the use of firearms; Paul had even earned a sharp-shooting medal during his tour of duty in peacetime Europe. But when Paul did buy a .22-caliber rifle that he kept in his bedroom closet with his dirty magazines—later upgrading to a .35-caliber Remington—the only creatures he ever shot, as far as I know, were squirrels and stray cats when he went upstate to visit his old army buddy, whom he called "The Don" and whom he credited with single-handedly reducing to zero the stray cat population of Syracuse.

Bobby in Naziland

When I visited Paul after he moved there, he and The Don took me small-game hunting, and I managed to wound a squirrel, which I then obliterated at point blank range with one more shot from the Remington—because I was 12 years old and boiling over with blood lust. But what really gives me a chill, when I think about that gray September afternoon, is that when Paul and The Don let me wander off on my own with the rifle, I was thinking that I'd like to shoot somebody, just to see what it felt like—I could say it was an accident. Instead, I aimed at nothing, firing a dozen rounds into the woods because it felt good to just shoot a gun.

The only guns my father ever bought were two antique flintlock pistols that he picked up for a few bucks in a flea market and then hung on his bedroom wall. As far as I know, if he ever fired these weapons at anybody, of any color, it was only in his dreams.

11

Fragments of My Father

Yes, my father wore his hatred on his sleeve like a badge of honor—because that's what he wanted people to see. He thought it made him look like a tough son of a bitch who was not to be fucked with, and maybe it did. But it was possible for certain people—like me, my mother, and perhaps a few others—to occasionally get beyond this facade, and if you managed to do that, what you'd find lurking just beneath the surface was a seething mass of contradictions.

I can, for example, picture my father one afternoon, in the summer of 1961, standing in front of his newly acquired, reddish-pink '58 Studebaker President, a proud step up from his '52 Oldsmobile 88. And he's telling me, in a tone of mild annoyance, that he will not put bumper stickers of any kind on this car because "they make the car look like hell."

When I press the matter, he says with growing irritation, "Only schmucks put bumper stickers on cars." And finally, in response to my unrelenting appeals, he explains, in exasperation, that bumper stickers could attract the attention of the police, who might dislike the sticker, even if it says something totally innocuous—like "Catskill Game Farm," which is the one I'm lobbying for because I want the world to know I've been to the Catskill Game Farm.

And it occurs to me now that my father, who firmly believed in the right of the police (and all other white men) to shoot on sight looters and rioters, feared and distrusted the police. He thought they were inherently corrupt and would need little pretext to again arrest him (or my grandfather) on vice charges, or, if they felt like it, pull him over on a deserted Brooklyn side street and shake him down for every penny he had on him—because they had something against the Catskill Game Farm.

It was around this same time that my father first told me, "Never sign a petition." Though I had no idea why he said this and he rarely took the trouble to explain himself to me (or anybody else), I now believe he thought signing virtually any petition was tantamount to being a Communist sympathizer. He was well aware of all the people whose lives had been ruined because, during the Depression, they had signed petitions for Communist Party candidates or for something as idealistic as world peace and were later accused of being Communists. Of course, some of them *were* Communists—like my namesake, Robert Rossen, the Academy Award–winning director who was born Robert *Rosen*, but added an extra "s" because he thought Rosen sounded too Jewish for Hollywood. Rossen, like so many others who'd joined the Communist Party in the 1930s was, 20 years later, subpoenaed to testify before the House Un-American Activities Committee, but he refused to name "fellow travelers." Then, despite having made a string of classic films, including *All the King's Men* and *Body and Soul*, Rossen (or Rosen) was blacklisted and remained unemployed for two years until, in a career-saving act of contrition my father would have found even more repulsive than being a Communist, he testified again and "ratted out" 57 current and former Communists. Hollywood then forgave Rossen, removed him from the blacklist, and permitted him to make *The Hustler*, with Paul Newman and Jackie Gleason.

If my father knew about Rossen, he never mentioned it to me. *Never sign a petition* appeared to be just another one of his imperious orders, unsupported by any rational evidence. Yet he said it so many times that on the rare occasions I have signed petitions, such as for a Democrat who wanted to run for City Council in New York, my father's words have floated back into my head, creating the tiniest nervous frisson.

He also told me, "Never wait in line for anything but money," an idea he apparently formulated in the crucible of the army. Can I do anything useful with this information? Has it ever stopped me from occasionally waiting in line to see a movie? No, it hasn't. But these words have the same effect as his petition-signing command. I stand in line wondering if I'm just another schmuck surrounded by schmucks who want to see a damn movie.

My father was always spouting dictums, absurd and otherwise. Yet there was another side of him, a side that showed itself one afternoon, circa 1956, in an event that springs to mind seemingly sepia-toned: We're sitting at the kitchen table in my grandmother Ruth's house, and as Ruth putters at the stove over a pot of her tasteless chicken soup, my father recites a poem to me, a silly poem that I love:

Fuzzy Wuzzy was a bear
Fuzzy Wuzzy had no hair
Fuzzy Wuzzy wasn't fuzzy, was he?

Laughing, I tell him, "Draw Uncle Squiggly! Draw Mister

Bobby in Naziland

Needlenose!"

Grabbing a pad and pencil that's lying by the telephone, he begins scratching out a menagerie of bug-eyed faces and weirdly shaped heads, some with one crazy hair popping out in the middle. And I can't imagine having a better time or being more entertained.

But this particular memory doesn't fit well into the jigsaw puzzle of who my father, in all his loving and bigoted glory, was. His sporadic ability to display tenderness ended around 1958, apparently killed off by 10 corrosive years of working in the candy store. And it was replaced by the cold and steely toughness that in later years he'd generally express with enraged threats to ship me off to military school if I didn't "straighten out," which I took to mean immediate, unquestioning, and total obedience to all parental demands.

Nevertheless, the surprising abundance of pleasant, bordering on happy, moments that endure in my mind is almost enough to make me forget about those threats. The afternoon of July 25, 1961 stands out:

It's two days before my birthday and, as it happens, two weeks before the birth of my brother. His name will be Jerrold, a subtle nod to my father's father, Julius—because not even my parents want to give the kid a name reminiscent of a man who died in the electric chair, and "Julius" is out of fashion, anyway. (I wanted to call him Jed, which I thought sounded cool, but my mother rejected it out of hand, because she said it was a "hillbilly name." She would have named the baby Jacqueline—as in Kennedy—had it been a girl.)

But it's not impending birth that's on my mind on this dazzling July day. It's baseball! My father has taken me to Yankee Stadium for my first major league game, a doubleheader against the Chicago White Sox. We have good seats in the grandstand, right behind third base, but the enormous ball park, the emerald green outfield, and the game itself look nothing like the black-and-white shadows I'm accustomed to seeing on TV. I'm so disoriented I can't follow the action and can barely see the ball. But I can see in the flesh all the Yankees I've been watching on TV for most of my life—Moose Skowron and Yogi Berra and Bobby Richardson and the great switch-hitter Mickey Mantle (my second-favorite Yankee) and Whitey Ford, who's pitching. I can hardly believe that I'm in the same ball park as they are, breathing the same air, and that I can hear the crack of the bat as my favorite Yankee, Roger Maris, on the road to 61 home runs, connects for numbers 37 and 38, and that I can see his face up close each time he rounds third base, head down, arms pumping, muscles bulging under his cutoff sleeves, looking like a man doing his job, showing no sense of the joy that I feel to just *be* in Yankee Stadium with my father on this summer afternoon.

Then there are those rare summer afternoons when, on my father's day off, we go to Brighton Beach or Manhattan Beach or even Riis Park, in Queens (though never to Coney Island because that's where the Negroes and Puerto Ricans go). I'm four years old, and with my mother trailing behind us, lugging our supplies, my father's carrying me across the scalding sand, picking his way through the forest of umbrellas, along narrow paths between blankets, the beach a wall-to-wall carpet of bronzing Brooklyn multitudes.

Sitting near the edge of the blanket, close to the water, where the sand is cool, I'm digging holes, digging tunnels, digging until I hit water, filling my pail with mud and turning it upside down, making a row of sand castles, and thinking that this tide I keep hearing about is the ocean foam, the suds from Tide detergent.

Bobby in Naziland

Then I look at my father—in his sunglasses and tight yellow swimming trunks, his taut, Coppertone-slick abs glistening as he smokes a cigarette and reads a paperback spy novel that he took from the candy store—with my mother sitting at his side, smoking and reading the newspaper.

A vendor in a pith helmet, ice chest slung over his shoulder, makes his way towards our blanket, singing out, over and over, "Get your ice cream here... ice-cold soda!"

"Can I have an ice cream?" I ask my father.

Before he can answer, my mother says, "When you get home, you can get one in the store."

My father says nothing.

It's a day of salt pills and the smell of suntan lotion, the inevitable sunburn, and my mother telling me to wait an interminable hour before I go in the water after I've eaten the tuna sandwich she's brought from home.

"Why do I have to wait so long?"

"Because if you don't, you'll get a cramp and drown."

I have no idea what a cramp is.

Finally, my lunch properly digested, with my father on one side and my mother on the other, I wade slowly into the gray seaweed-and-garbage-strewn waters, the two of them urging me to "get wet already."

"It's too cold," I protest, thinking about the framed colorized photo, on the dresser in their bedroom, taken on their honeymoon in Miami Beach. The water there is turquoise, the sand golden, and every time I see that picture, I think Miami is the most beautiful city in the world, a magical place where the ocean, unlike the bracing surf of Brighton Beach or Riis Park, is a soothing bath that requires no "getting used to," and the sun is so strong that, as my mother often tells me, "you can only take it for 15 minutes at first—you have to be very careful."

My God, how I want to go to Miami! But talk about impossible dreams. In 1957, around the time I grasp the concept of a state called Florida, traveling anywhere more exotic than Poughkeepsie seems as fantastic as space flight. Miami, like Manhattan, might as well be Oz—a Technicolor fantasyland, where, if I'm lucky, I might get to someday in the distant future, but only briefly, and only to return to a black-and-white Brooklyn with one colorized photo to prove I was there.

And at last I dip my entire body into the gray waters of Brighton Beach, yelping because it's so damn cold.

The fragments of my father that comprised the routine domesticity of life on East 17th Street always return with the melancholy glow of all things tainted by the candy store: I see him at the kitchen table, still in his candy-store clothes—blue button-down shirt, chinos, and heavy black work boots—eating borscht and sour cream, or gefilte fish with horseradish, or knaidlach (matzo balls) and milk, or schav, a greenish herb soup. After work, my father likes to eat "Jewish foods," which, despite my mother's urging—"Just a spoonful!"—I refuse to taste because most of them, especially the schav, look disgusting.

In fact, it's a bowl of schav he's eating the afternoon he instigates my first act of violence: I'm four, and I come running into the apartment, crying.

"What's wrong?" he asks, looking up from the steaming green concoction before him.

"Howard Kaplan punched me!" I say of the kid who lives on the second floor.

"Did you hit him back?"

"No."

Bobby in Naziland

"Well, go downstairs and hit him back. Then he'll leave you alone."

So I go downstairs and smash my toy rifle over Howard Kaplan's head, breaking the plastic gun in two.

Howard begins blubbering hysterically, and I run back upstairs to tell my father what I've done. He's very proud of me, he says, now enjoying a cigarette after having finished his meal. Blowing a smoke ring, he then suggests that in the future, I hit people with my fists rather than my toys. I promise him that I'll do this—and it's a promise I keep.

Because just as my father had predicted, Howard Kaplan never bothered me again; in fact, he ran away every time he saw me coming. It also proved to be the only piece of advice he ever gave me that actually worked—at least with Howard Kaplan. In years to come, though, I often found his suggestions dispiriting—like "Go to West Point and get an engineering degree. Then you can go into the army as a second lieutenant"; or "You're not going to make any money as a writer, so if you want a steady job, work in the post office."

Such counsel, I thought, demonstrated a complete lack of understanding of who I was or what I wanted my life to be. But it did show his concern for my less than promising financial future.

Being a true believer in free enterprise, my father was forever coming up with moneymaking schemes for everybody, especially himself. So dedicated was he to the idea of getting rich quick (or at any speed), on his dying day he was still working on a scheme that he'd revealed to me two years earlier, in the autumn of 2003. I was unpacking my bags in the guestroom of my parents' condo in the retirement community where they now lived, outside

Palm Beach, when he told me that he wasn't exactly retired. He wanted to be an entrepreneur again, he said, and he was going to get back into the game with a new product he'd come up with, Innuendo.

"It started out as a wrinkle cream," he explained, handing me a sample. "But then we thought we'd make more money if we sold it to gay people as an anal lubricant."

"Who's 'we'?" I asked, amazed that he used the word "gay" (not to mention "anal"), perhaps indicating a partial retreat from the aggressive hatred of everyone and everything different that had once consumed him. I was even more amazed that Innuendo—*was it a pun?*—already existed, as did the jar it came in.

"My old friend Manny," he said, "you know, from Brooklyn. He lives down here now. He made a fortune in gold futures—he's backing me."

"Well, good luck," I said as I studied the white porcelain container and the jaunty, professionally designed label—though I didn't understand why, of all things under the subtropical sun, my father, still reaching for the golden ring at the age of 80, had decided he wanted to be the anal-lube king of South Florida. And I wondered, despite these tentative signs of mellowing, perhaps brought on by semi-retirement and the velvety Palm Beach warmth, how many gay people there could possibly be in South Florida (or on Planet Earth, for that matter) who'd buy any sex product from my "tough son of a bitch," law-and-order Republican father, who'd declared George W. Bush a traitor because he'd once come to Florida and given a speech in Spanish.

Which may (or may not) explain why Project Innuendo never got beyond the prototype phase.

12

Maris in the Fall

With the transistor radio pressed to my ear, I can feel the electricity of 25,000 people in Dodger Stadium and a million more who are tuned in coast-to-coast. I can feel it pouring into Maury Wills, surging through his body. The Dodger infielder, having drawn yet another walk against the Chicago Cubs, takes a huge lead off first base, and the frenzied L.A. crowd, knowing he's feeding off their energy, is on its feet, chanting "Go, Maury, go!" willing him to fly, to again steal second, now only 80 feet away.

I, too, from 2,500 miles away, want Maury to go. And I know he *will* go—at the right moment. Everybody knows it... because he always does. And then, as the Cubs pitcher reaches the point of no return in his windup, Maury accelerates like a gazelle and dives head-first into second base, kicking up a cloud of dust as the throw from the catcher sails over the leaping shortstop's outstretched glove, into center field. Maury jumps to his feet, sprints towards third, pulls in standing up, and the Dodger fans roar even louder, urging him to steal home.

It's amazing how Maury Wills does it every time. Nobody

can throw him out, not in this magical season, and not on this bright and gritty August afternoon, in 1962, as I stroll across the the dead grass and red dust of the Parade Grounds, the sacred turf on which my favorite Dodger, *Jewish* strikeout king Sandy Koufax—injured last month and out for the rest of the year, but not before throwing a no-hitter against the atrocious New York Mets—was nurtured and groomed for greatness.

What am I supposed to do, listen to the Mets, the new team in town, created out of thin air to replace the irreplaceable Brooklyn Dodgers? Not a chance.

I'm going to listen to the L.A. Dodgers whenever I can find one of their games on my radio. And currently the Dodgers, handily disposing of the ninth-place Cubs, are locked in a late-season life-and-death struggle with the San Francisco Giants (that other team that deserted New York for California) for the National League pennant and the right to lose the World Series to my favorite team, the invincible Yankees.

My heart beats faster at the sound of Vin Scully's voice, clear and resonant as it comes over the radio, his excitement bubbling just beneath the calm and precise enunciation. Listening to Scully is almost as exciting as listening to Yankees broadcaster Mel Allen shout "Going... going... *gone!*" every time a Bronx Bomber blasts one into the bleachers. Scully satisfies a vestigial longing deep in my soul, as well as in the soul of every Brooklynite who never got over the Dodgers.

And why shouldn't it? I belonged to the last generation that would have a living connection to the Brooklyn Dodgers. Conceived in October 1951, in the delirious aftermath of Bobby Thomson's Dodger-destroying home run, I was born at Beth El Hospital, practically in the shadow of Ebbets Field. Had this occurred even a couple of months later, I would not have been old enough, while growing up, to bond with the team and form a distinct memory of them that I'd carry with me for the rest of my life. The Dodger logo was veritably tattooed on my ass when the doctor delivered his "life-giving" slap, and then my mother, who bled Dodger Blue, named me Robert—supposedly after her uncle, an "adventurer" who went off to fight in the Spanish Civil War and never came back... *Missing in action, presumed dead*— though everybody called me Bobby, which would always carry echoes of Thomson, whether my parents had intended it or not.

Yes, I remember watching the Dodgers on the tiny screen of our black-and-white TV, among my mother and her friends, both male and female, who'd gather in the living room for an afternoon of cheering on and despairing over "Them Bums." And I remember running around the room repeating, as my mother had taught me to say (to everyone's great amusement), "The Giants make doody in their pants!" every time the Dodgers played their despised Polo Grounds rivals. Yes, I remember Jackie Robinson, Duke Snider, Gil Hodges, and Roy Campanella infusing the household with their underdog Brooklyn excitement, even as they lost the seventh game of the 1956 World Series—taking place a mile away at Ebbets Field—9-0, to the Yankees. And I remember when, the following year, right after I'd started kindergarten, "that son of a bitch" Walter O'Malley (whoever he was) snatched away the Dodgers in the middle of the night, before my own passion had had a chance to blossom into maturity.

To me, the Dodgers, now my second-favorite team, were like a phantom limb—they were gone but I could feel them. And my second-favorite Dodger, Maury Wills, a speed demon on the base paths, was like a new Jackie Robinson, minus the politics but just as black. I had a profound appreciation for Wills's genius at getting on base. Though a sub-.300 hitter, he used his blazing speed to force errors, turn routine ground balls into singles, turn walks into triples (as he'd just done against the Cubs), and rattle the pitcher into committing balks. It was electrifying when he got on base and the cat-and-mouse game began, with Wills inching further and further from the bag. Everybody in the stadium (especially the pitcher), everybody listening on the radio, everybody watching on TV knew he was going to steal— second, then third, and possibly even home—and in 1962, he'd do it *104 times*, breaking Ty Cobb's record of 96 steals, which had stood for 47 years.

Unlike my main man, Roger Maris, and his powerfully built teammate Mickey Mantle, I knew *I* was never going to hit a lot of home runs. That's why Wills's steals were an athletic feat I could relate to. When I played baseball, even as I swung for the fences, I was lucky to make contact with the ball and delighted on the rare occasions I beat out an infield roller. I was a lousy hitter (and a worse fielder). But someday, I thought, I might steal a lot of bases, like Maury Wills—if I could only figure out how to get on base more often... and then find a pickup game at the Parade Grounds where the ground rules permitted stealing, which they never did, not in any game I'd ever played in. The brutal simplicity of football—just take the ball and run—was the only game in which I'd been able to apply my own speed-demon talents. Baseball, a sport that required subtlety and precision, simply didn't lend itself to my undisciplined skills; to learn baseball was a struggle. And that's why I admired the professional athletes who played the game so beautifully.

Few things gave me more pleasure than listening to baseball and football on the little blue transistor radio that my parents had given me for my ninth birthday. I enjoyed it even more than watching the games on TV—because it was *my* radio, and I could

Bobby in Naziland

take it with me anywhere, like the Parade Grounds, even though I knew I was putting myself in grave danger of it being stolen. Or I could hide away in my room and listen to anything at all as I sorted through my baseball cards, which is what I was doing the day my mother ran into the room to tell me what she'd just heard on the kitchen radio: Adolf Eichmann had been found guilty of crimes against humanity and had been sentenced to hang.

But I already knew that. I'd heard it on *my* radio at the top of the hour. And it was through that radio that the perpetual stream of information now filtered into my consciousness. Unlike TV, radio seemed amorphous. There were dozens of stations; some only came in at night. Anything could be anywhere anytime. I never knew what I might find as I scanned up and down the dial until a bit of news or music caught my ear: the X-15 rocketing to the very edge of outer space, at 4,000 miles per hour... Wilt "The Stilt" Chamberlain pouring in a hundred points against the hapless New York Knicks... Jimmy Dean singing "Big Bad John"... or the Ranger 4 spacecraft crash-landing on the dark side of the moon but failing to send back the close-up photos of the lunar surface I'd so badly wanted to see—a failure I took personally as an American, resulting in a free-floating sadness that I couldn't shake for weeks.

This is what I lost myself in, in the days and months just before and after the birth of my brother, Jerrold, on August 8, 1961. It's not that I tuned out the reality of the new baby who'd taken up residence in a used bassinette in my parents' bedroom. Rather, I felt somehow outside that reality, as if what was happening in the house had nothing to do with me. Ever since April or so I'd been watching my mother's belly grow, and on occasion I was allowed to feel the baby kicking inside her. Then he came into the world bearing a miniaturized approximation

110

of my father's face, and after a couple of days at Maimonides Hospital, where a nurse had held him up to the window so I could see for the first time this tiny thing in a diaper, he was loaded into the Studebaker and driven home.

How odd, I thought, to have a baby brother after nine years of being an only child, of thinking I'd always be an only child and that it might be fun if I had a playmate, an ally, someone to take the edge off my isolation when that isolation became too much. But now that I had one, I wasn't quite sure how much I wanted things to change. In my own bedroom at the opposite end of the apartment, with my new transistor radio for company, I did my best to ignore the ongoing commotion—a commotion that reached a barbaric crescendo on the eighth day of Jerrold's *Jewish* life, the day of his *bris*. That's when a *mohel*—a bearded rabbi in a black coat and black felt hat—came to the house carrying his instruments in a black case, like a doctor, and with a throng of friends and relatives crowded around Jerrold's bassinette, which had been moved into the living room for the holy occasion, the rabbi proceeded to slice off my brother's foreskin. I couldn't bear to watch. It was too horrible. And I couldn't help grabbing my own penis in sympathetic agony when I heard him scream, which he continued to do throughout the day before his screaming finally faded into subdued whimpering, after my parents brought Jerrold and his bassinette into my room. They wanted me to keep an eye on him while everybody feasted on the Jewish foods—the *challah*, chopped liver, and gefilte fish, spread out in the living room on a big metal folding table my parents had rented for the foreskin party.

Over the next couple of months, in the confined space of my own room, I ignored the feeding, burping, diapering, bathing, and everything else that was required to keep the new baby alive and healthy. It was more work than having a pet, I thought. Yes, of course I'd go look at my brother (and his circumcised penis) every so often, lying there in the bassinette, wiggling around, apparently recovered from the religious trauma the rabbi had so recently inflicted upon him. In fact, with the notable exception of his bris day, Jerrold was a mostly quiet addition to the household, a "good baby," as people said, one who didn't shriek all night the way I had, as my mother now liked to remind me.

"When we brought *you* home from the hospital, you screamed your head off every night," she said. "You'd stop when we picked you up, but as soon as we put you down, you'd start screaming again. The doctor told us to just ignore you, and you'd eventually stop. We'd lie in bed listening to you scream for hours. But he was right. You finally stopped."

Ah, I thought, somebody new for my mother to compare me to.

Not that it was Jerrold's fault. I liked Jerrold. Sometimes I'd pick him up, carry him around, listen to him happily gurgling and cooing—all that "good baby" stuff he did. But I usually left him alone because there wasn't much to talk about with an infant who hadn't learned to talk yet. And with each passing day, I came to value even more the privacy of my room, where I'd hole up for entire afternoons and nights while my father logged even more candy store hours—another mouth to feed—and my mother focused virtually all her attention on the new baby, which, I soon realized, left her significantly less time to harass me, thus making Jerrold a good thing. His demanding presence allowed me to spend more time than ever before in peace, behind closed doors, nurturing my obsessions, looking at my baseball cards, studying slides under my microscope, looking out my window at the moon through my telescope, trying to build a robot with my Erector set, listening to my transistor radio, and ignoring as much as possible the new living creature who'd joined the household—at least until he was old enough to crawl into my room, which was still a year off.

But as that long-ago summer of 1961 faded into autumn, it was the magnetic pull of Roger Maris and his pursuit of Babe Ruth's "unbreakable" home run record that would become my #1 obsession, often the only thing I could or wanted to think about. Not only would I soon be licking the sidewalk 61 times in front of Jeffrey Abromovitz's house in exchange for his rare Maris baseball card, but my father had allowed me to get a Roger Maris flattop crew cut that was such an oddity, my classmates would ask if they could touch it. And for my birthday, my grandmother Ruth bought me a Roger Maris bat, the first baseball bat I'd ever owned, *and* a Roger Maris glove, a significant upgrade from my father's decrepit hand-me-down fielder's mitt, though neither one improved my hitting or fielding.

My attraction to Maris probably crossed over into the realm of the homoerotic—not that I was aware that such a thing existed or had a name. All I knew was that the sight of Maris or anything associated with him—his baseball card, his name on my glove and bat, his picture in the newspaper, his image on TV, and especially that one time I saw him live and in-person at Yankee Stadium—was thrilling. And his epic quest to break Babe Ruth's record, with Mickey Mantle launching moon shots right behind him, was the most exciting thing I'd ever witnessed (with the possible exception of the Project Mercury astronauts' blasting into space).

My brother wasn't quite two months old when Maris pulled to within striking distance of Ruth's record, hitting number 59, against the Baltimore Orioles, on a night I had to write a

Bobby in Naziland

book report.

"You need to concentrate on what you're doing or you'll never get into college," my mother reminded me as she confiscated my transistor radio, which she knew I listened to when I did homework. (That was one reason she'd recently dragged me to a child psychologist, who, despite administering a battery of standardized tests, had failed to determine why I had such an alarming lack of desire to concentrate on schoolwork, which, the psychologist said, was the root cause of my chronic "underachieving"—as if it took a psychologist to figure that one out.)

So I didn't find out about the home run until the next day, when I read about it in the *Daily News*, "New York's picture newspaper," according to its slogan. This was a misnomer, our teacher, Mrs. Haber, had told us. The *Times* actually had more pictures; she'd counted them. The pictures in the *News* were just bigger.

And a big picture of Maris did, indeed, accompany the article, which noted that there were still eight games to go in the regular season. I found that reassuring. That was plenty of time for him to put two or even three more into the seats.

But all he managed over the course of the next three games were a couple of base hits.

On the night of September 26, as my mother and I were driving home from my grandmother Helen's house, she was letting me listen to the Yankee game, again against Baltimore, on the car radio. Phil Rizzuto was calling the play-by-play, and just as Maris came to bat for the second time, in the bottom of the third, with two out, nobody on, and the Orioles leading 2-0, she pulled into the bus stop in front of the candy store and, leaving the engine running and the radio on, told me to wait in the car while she went inside to argue with my father about God knows what.

Jack Fisher, the Baltimore pitcher, got two quick strikes on Maris. That's when I heard the excitement level rise in Rizzuto's voice, and I knew what was going to happen next. Rizzuto must have seen an almost undetectable adjustment in Maris's stance, in his body language. I'd seen that sort of thing myself a number of times when I was watching a game on TV and I'd just know that the batter, whoever it was, was going to hit one out—and then he did.

Sure enough, Fisher threw Maris the fastball he was waiting for. I heard the crack of the bat, and then the roar pouring from the radio, drowning out Rizzuto, as the ball sailed deep into the right-field seats.

Jumping out of the car, I ran up to the store and called to my parents through the front window, "Roger Maris just hit number 60! He tied Babe Ruth!"

My mother stopped arguing with my father just long enough to say, "Get back in the car before we get a $25 ticket!"

So I did. And the Yanks came from behind to win, though Maris failed to hit another home run that night.

I couldn't believe it when, the next day, Yankee manager Ralph Houk said that Maris needed a rest and benched him for the next game. How could he do that with only three games left in the regular season?

In the two games that followed, the opposing pitchers gave Maris nothing to hit, walking him time and again.

By Sunday, October 1, the final day of the regular season, my confidence in Roger Maris had evaporated. I was positive that just as the experts had been saying all along, he wasn't going to break Ruth's record. Nobody was going to let him. The record, sacrosanct, had stood unassailed for 34 years. In my lifetime, nobody before Maris had ever hit more than 52 home runs—Mantle had done it in 1956, a feat that I barely remembered. When I checked the *Information Please Almanac*, I saw that even the great New York (and San Francisco) Giant, Willie Mays, had never hit more than 51—he did that in 1955, before I was fully conscious of a thing called major league baseball. And the last time anybody had come close to Ruth was *1938*, when Hebrew Hammer Hank Greenberg of the Detroit Tigers hit 58 home runs.

So forget about it, I thought—history was not going to be made; that much was clear. And that's why I had no intention of sitting home all afternoon and watching the game—against the Red Sox, a lousy team, 33 games out of first place. The Yanks had already won 108 games, and in a couple of days they were going to the World Series to play the Cincinnati Reds. There was nothing left to be decided and there would be nothing to see. The game was a "tune-up"; that's what everybody was calling it.

All right, so maybe I did watch the first inning on TV and saw that Yankee Stadium was half-empty, with a bunch of die-hard fans filling only the lower deck in right field, the spot where most of Maris's home runs landed—not because they believed he was going to hit one, but because they wanted to be there on the off chance he did. After all, there was a *$5,000 bounty* on the ball, enough money in 1961 to live well for a year or longer. But when Maris flied out to left, to Boston's one legitimate star, Carl Yastrzemski, that only confirmed what I knew. *It's not going to happen. Not today.* Maris, a classic left-handed pull hitter, almost never homered to left field. He wasn't getting around on the Boston pitcher, Tracy Stallard, who had no intention of serving up anything good.

Around 2:30, I decided to walk over to the Parade Grounds,

without my radio, figuring I'd watch a couple of sandlot clubs in action, maybe the Tomahawks, Sandy Koufax's old team. I'd do what I always did: stand five feet behind home plate, with my nose pressed to the chain-link backstop, and observe the umpire grunting his ball and strike calls, and the catcher chattering "No batter... no batter..." as the pitcher threw hopping fastballs and hard-breaking balls, the likes of which I wondered if I'd ever be able to touch, even with my Roger Maris bat.

It was about a quarter to three when I crossed Caton Avenue and spotted, on the corner of Parade Place, Barry Gardner's mother, Priscilla, sitting alone on a park bench, listening to the Yankee game on a big black transistor radio—a much nicer one than mine—and eating a sandwich. She waved to me and I walked over.

It was the bottom of the fourth inning, still no score.

"Maris is coming up again," Priscilla said. "Think he'll do it?"

I shook my head but thought I'd hang out for a few minutes anyway, just to make sure.

Standing behind the bench, I listened to the play-by-play as Stallard made quick work of the leadoff hitter, shortstop Tony Kubeck, striking him out. Then Phil Rizzuto's voice rose to a higher pitch. "Here comes Roger Maris!" he said. "They're standing up, waiting to see if he's going to hit number 61."

And the Yankee fans made such a racket, it sounded as if the half-empty "House that Ruth Built" were packed to the rafters.

The first pitch to "Roger," as Rizzuto called him, was "way outside... ball one."

The crowd booed, demanding Stallard give him something to hit.

"Low," said Rizzuto, "ball two. That one was in the dirt."

Bobby in Naziland

The booing grew louder, more frantic.

"*Fastball hit deep to right,*" Rizzuto shrieked on the next pitch. "*Way back there... holy cow! What a shot!*"

I could picture it as clearly as if I were watching it on TV, as Rizzuto described, over the unearthly sound of a crowd gone berserk, how people in the right-field seats were climbing all over each other, fighting for the ball and its $5,000 bounty.

"He did it!" I said to Priscilla. "He hit 61!"

"I knew he would," she said. "You know how you can just feel it sometimes?"

I did. And I ran home to watch TV. There it was on every channel, a loop playing over and over. I couldn't get enough of it: Red Barber this time calling the play-by-play... the madding mob in the right-field stands and the well-to-do spectators, in their jackets and ties, in the expensive seats, behind the dugout, everybody on their feet as Maris stands at home plate, waiting... then the pitch... the smooth, rhythmic swing... the crack of the bat as he connects... the spine-tingling roar of the crowd as the ball sails into the seats... and Maris, trotting around the bases, head down, muscled arms pumping under his cut-off sleeves, just as I remembered him from two months earlier, when I'd seen him hit numbers 37 and 38 in Yankee Stadium. He touches home plate, heads towards the dugout, past Yogi Berra, forgotten in the on-deck circle... and Maris emerges from the dugout for a curtain call, waving to the crowd, who can't believe what they've seen... he's taken off his cap, and there's his flattop crew cut, just like mine... and the Yanks win the game 1-0, Maris's homer providing the only score. Soon they identify the guy who caught the $5,000 ball: Sal Durante, 19, from Coney Island. And the next day, his picture fills the front page of the *Daily News*—Durante posing with the famous ball *and* Roger Maris—"The Rajah"—who has allowed himself to grin, to display a moment of public happiness in his accomplishment.

I was happy, too—for me, for Maris, and even for Durante. I was feeling that fleeting sense of "everything's coming up roses" (as the song went), of being alive in America when Yankees were breaking "unbreakable" records and Americans were being launched into outer space. It was a feeling that I wanted to share with my brother—that's what he was for, wasn't he? But he, too, lived in his own world, one beyond language, where things like Roger Maris, home runs, Yankees, and baseball itself meant nothing.

Besides, a few days later, locked in the sanctuary of my room, I noticed that that happiness, or whatever it was I had been feeling, was gone, vanished into thin air as if it had never happened.

Six months later, it would again flicker to life on the opening day of the baseball season, when my mother handed me the magazine section of the Sunday *Times*, open to a two-page spread of parody poems celebrating baseball. One asked, simply, why people go "to ball games with a radio."

Another, a paean (more than 10 years after the fact) to the hero of the never-to-be-forgotten Giant-Dodger playoff game of 1951, described how Bobby Thomson used his bat to knock "the Brooklyn Dodgers flat."

And two of the poems, along with the drawings that accompanied them, were goosebump-raising love fests paying homage to the man who'd hit 61. One, titled "The Last Time I Saw Maris," expressed the poet's love of the way Maris's bat came "'round," "smote the ball," and made a "shot-like sound."

Another, titled "Maris in the Spring" and borrowing from the

Bobby in Naziland

famous Paris song, again proclaimed the poet's undying love for Maris, in the springtime and the fall.

These tributes suggested that maybe I wasn't the only one in New York who'd lick the sidewalk for a Roger Maris baseball card. And for one fleetingly existential moment, as I began to read all the poems out loud and commit them to memory, I felt that maybe I wasn't alone in the universe, that there was at least one person out there somewhere—*New York Times* poet Milton Bracker (whoever he was)—who felt the same things I did and was able to so eloquently express (as I thought then) those feelings in the pages of a newspaper.

Someday, I thought, I want to write poems like these.

13

Cruel Affections

"You're wrong!" she said with the authority of a woman who could knock off the Sunday *Times* crossword puzzle—in pen—in under an hour. "*Irregardless* is *not* a word. The word is *regardless*!"

"Yes it *is* a word," my father disagreed, as he emerged from the bedroom, ready to leave for work. "*Irregardless* of what you think."

Trailing him down the foyer, her voice rising in shrillness and volume, my mother repeated, "*Irregardless* is *not* a word!" and proceeded to elaborate on her theories of correct usage—until my father walked out the door and shut it behind him, thus ending this unusual argument... unusual not because they were arguing, but because somebody was demonstrably right. And if either one of them had taken a moment to consult the dictionary, as I did afterwards—the dictionary that I'd recently learned my way around, struggling with a word-derivation assignment that nearly drove me to tears as I pored over the tiny type, trying to make sense of all the crazy symbols and abbreviations—they'd have found out that *irregardless* is a word, though a "nonstandard" one, at least according to Webster's.

Bobby in Naziland

But who was right and who was wrong was beside the point. Because even if I'd told them what I'd found in the dictionary, they'd have started arguing about the meaning of *nonstandard*, and my mother would have told my father, in her inimitable way, "Only uneducated people use nonstandard words!" Or they'd have found another word to argue about. There were hundreds of thousands to choose from, in a variety of languages.

My parents argued about stuff like this all the time because they enjoyed arguing, and that's all there was to it. At least that's the way it looked to me. I mean, what do you expect when my mother, a liberal-leaning Democrat (she didn't say "nigger") and true-blue Dodger fan, who loved the way Jackie Robinson danced off third base before stealing home, was bound by a till-death-do-us-part marriage to a Dodger-and-Jackie-Robinson-hating law-and-order Republican, and a Giant fan, whom she could never forgive for buying a candy store?

You expect two people who are going to argue, usually at high volume, about *everything*, no matter how trivial. And you expect that their arguments are going to become the background and foreground noise to their life, which happens to include me. And you expect that if my father isn't around to scream at, which is most of the time, then my mother is going scream at me instead—because I'm there.

There's a photograph of me, at age four, standing in my grandmother's bedroom and looking at the camera, a Kodak Brownie Hawkeye, in a state of deer-in-the-headlights shock. Every time I see that picture, it reminds me how, just before she snapped it, my mother was yelling at me: "Smile naturally! You always photograph horribly!"

That's what she said every time she took my picture, apparently never realizing that she made me so nervous, it was impossible to smile at all—which is why she hated every picture she ever took of me. And she was always worried about "wasting film," because it was so expensive to develop. But, I now know, the real reason she screamed had nothing to do with my inability to smile or the cost of film. She screamed because she wanted everything in her life to instantaneously change for the better, and she knew it wasn't going to happen—because nothing ever seemed to change. Every day was just like the one before it—not horrible in that Holocaust/terminal cancer kind of way, but not especially good, either.

Yet God help me when I'd tell my mother, "I wish we lived in a nicer apartment and had more money."

"Be thankful you have your health," she'd say, the toxic edge in her voice communicating her belief that I was a child ungrateful for what I did have.

Which was true. My mother knew I took my health for granted. And she knew that, just as she did, I longed to live in a beautiful apartment, preferably one with a terrace. And she knew that I scoured the real estate classifieds in *The New York Times* every Sunday, searching for that beautiful apartment for the $135 a month I was told we could afford. And she knew I'd never find it. Because such an apartment didn't exist. Not in Brooklyn. Certainly not one with a terrace.

It's no mystery what originally attracted my mother to my father. In pictures taken around the time they began dating, in 1947, he looked dangerous, in that irresistible James Dean kind of way, all slicked-back hair, cool aviator shades, and ever-present cigarette dangling from his lips. And judging by those same pictures, it's not hard to figure out what attracted him to her. I suspect my mother's many suitors—an army lieutenant among them—described her as a curvaceous brunette, or words to that effect. My mother and father both looked pretty hot.

If I were to venture a guess as to what mysterious force held them together for 56 years, until my father's death, then I'd go with a sort of sadomasochistic love—which is what they smothered me in, as well. My mother, in particular, doled out her affections—the occasional hug and kiss, or the sentence spoken in a pleasant and non-accusatory tone—only on those rare days when I obeyed her without question or brought home sterling marks on my report card. And whatever emotion I felt in return was probably more akin to Stockholm syndrome than love, and was grounded in the fear that if my parents didn't stop smoking cigarettes, then I'd end up an orphan like the Rosenberg kids. Which is why I told them daily, in that tone of contemptuous and unassailable authority that I'd learned from my mother, "You're both going to die from lung cancer if you don't stop smoking."

They didn't exactly argue with me about the validity of my prophecy. But my father, who had long ago turned my mother on to cigarettes to "calm her down," would tell me that he'd been smoking since he was in the army and enjoyed it too much to quit.

"It's too hard to quit," my mother would add. "One day you'll understand."

In desperation, I decided to hide my mother's cigarettes—I didn't have the nerve to hide my father's. But instead of throwing up her hands in defeat and renouncing tobacco on the spot, as I'd hoped she'd do, she cursed God and all that was holy as she tore apart the apartment until she found my hiding place; I'd wedged her cigarettes into the back of a kitchen cabinet.

"It's an addiction," she said sheepishly, lighting her Belair with trembling hands.

Still, there were two things I liked very much about my parents' cigarette-smoking: One was my father's Zippo lighter, which he'd had since the war, and that I loved to play with—flip it open, flick the wheel, ignite the wick, and just stare at the flame. The other was the fact that both my mother's Belairs and my father's Raleighs came with "valuable coupons" redeemable for "free gifts." And because my father sold vast quantities of both brands in the candy store, he got four additional coupons every time he opened a carton to restock the shelves. We accumulated thousands of coupons, and it was my special joy to look through the gift catalogues to see what we could redeem them for, though the stuff I really wanted—a sports car, a speedboat, a Piper Cub—required *millions* of coupons, and I didn't understand how anybody (or any family) could smoke that many cigarettes.

Without my prodding, my parents redeemed their coupons for a portable typewriter, and they gave it to me, on no particular occasion and, as far as I could see, with no strings attached.

About two weeks later, they both stopped smoking, cold turkey, never to pick up another cigarette.

I'd witnessed a miracle, I thought, as I began to teach myself to type.

Twenty-five years later, I'd still be typing on that little blue Olivetti.

14

In America...

... everybody's equal.
... there's no royalty.
... there's no class distinction.
... anyone can grow up to be president.

Well, maybe that last one is theoretically true—for anybody with the wherewithal to raise a billion dollars. But I used to believe they were *all* true, because that's what my mother taught me and that's what they taught us in school—by making us face the American flag, place our hand over our heart, and repeat daily that we lived in "one nation, under God... with liberty and justice for all."

Though it didn't take me that long to figure out that the notion of America as a country of equality, without royalty, was pure propaganda—was Elvis not the King?—it wasn't until early 2010, some 35 years after I fled Flatbush, that I saw the inherent absurdity of telling a kid growing up on East 17th Street that there was no class distinction.

It just hit me one day that a line as bright and clear as an international boundary ran down the middle of that street. It separated the middle class from the lower middle class, and my mother knew better than anybody that we lived on the wrong side of this class divide. The American class system, the one I'd been taught didn't exist, had placed us firmly within the confines of the candy-store class, and every time my mother walked outside, East 17th Street rubbed her nose in it. Our side of the street, the odd-numbered side, though not exactly a slum, was lined with semi-dilapidated apartment buildings, all of them distinctly shabbier than the stately, well-maintained monuments to middle-class prosperity that lined the other side of the street.

Ironically, all the odd-numbered buildings had classy-sounding British names, like Caton Arms and Brighton Hall, which was the one I lived in. But they weren't intended as ironic. When these apartment houses were built, around 1930, they *were* classy buildings, the hallways decorated with finely carved Corinthian columns and marble fireplaces (now sealed off)—vestiges of an earlier time, before the Depression and a quarter-century of landlord neglect had taken its toll.

Though it never occurred to me that I was living on the wrong side of the street—or that there was a wrong side of the street—I was well aware that I was living in a quasi-slum and I even knew why: because we had no money. My parents, lacking neither ambition nor intelligence, understood just how hard it was going to be to earn enough money to emerge from the candy-store class and fulfill my mother's fantasy of a split-level house in a suburban subdivision and a husband who was a respected professional *anything*, both of which she believed she was entitled to by Jewish law.

In the meantime, she did what she could to make our apartment "look decent," devoting a major portion of each day

Bobby in Naziland

to vacuuming, mopping, waxing, scrubbing, scouring, dusting, or polishing every floor, wall, window, fixture, and stick of furniture in our four shabby rooms, until she became the very embodiment of the biblical proverb "Cleanliness is next to godliness." And she believed that the end result of her relentless efforts was a house so immaculate that anytime I dropped food on the floor, I could pick it up and eat it.

"I just mopped the floor," she'd say. "It's clean."

Which was true. She'd *always* just mopped the floor. And I always ate any food I dropped on the floor, thereby becoming the avatar of her ultimate compliment: "Her house is so clean you can eat off the floor," which she often said of her mother, Helen, whose home smelled faintly of bleach because she was forever scrubbing everything with Clorox to "kill the germs."

But it just wasn't possible to make our house sparkle like the ones my mother saw on TV, because no matter what she cleaned or how often she cleaned it, there was no disguising the fact that even if Mister Clean himself had come down like Jesus from heaven and unleashed a "white tornado," nothing could ever restore the apartment to the state of virgin pristinity to which she aspired. The peeling paint, crumbling plaster, splintered wooden floors, broken tiles, cracked bathroom fixtures, and persistent lack of heat and hot water (courtesy of our incompetent super, Mr. Kruger), which forced us on cold days to huddle around the stove as if it were a hearth and boil water to take baths, all conspired to reaffirm a simple truth: Nothing could hold impending squalor at bay.

That's just the way it had been since we'd moved in, in 1953. Yet every time my mother saw a fingerprint on the wall, you'd think we were living in the grand palace of Versailles—she'd come streaking down the foyer, sponge in hand, shrieking hysterically, "Why can't you walk without touching the walls?" and then attack the offending smudge as if possessed by the demon of domestic purity.

I can see my mother with a cigarette in her mouth and a vacuum-cleaner hose in her hand, her space-agey Lewyt trailing behind and emitting a piercing howl as it sucks up dirt and crumbs from the threadbare living-room carpet—the one she sits on Saturday nights watching *Perry Mason* and playing solitaire while my father works in the candy store around the corner. And I see myself, fingers in my ears as I flee the room, begging her, "Mommy, please, turn the vacuum *off*! I can't stand the noise anymore!" Or I can see her on that carpet knitting a sweater for me, or on her knees, cutting fabric with pinking shears so she can sew an evening dress for herself that she says she can't afford to buy in a store because it would cost hundreds of dollars. Or I can see her at the kitchen sink, washing dishes as I dry them, one of the regular chores I'm obligated to perform every night immediately after dinner, to earn my 50-cent-a-week allowance and to ensure that we don't give the roaches an opportunity to feast on dirty dishes piled up in the sink—because the roaches are so out of control, when you turn on the kitchen light at night, the room comes alive with them, a roiling brown carpet covering every surface, then vanishing instantaneously. (Nothing can kill them—not a full can of Black Flag, not a professional exterminator, and probably not a nuclear weapon.) My mother always said that the worst thing a housekeeper could do—the cosmic opposite of keeping a house so clean you could eat off the floor—was to let dishes pile up in the sink.

"You walk into the kitchen and the first thing you see is a sink full of dirty dishes," she'd say, usually about some hapless goy neighbor, as if this were the most humiliating tragedy that could possibly befall a housewife. "If you want a drink of water, she has to dig around in the sink until she finds a glass, and then she has to wash it out. Can you imagine living in a house like that?"

Actually, I couldn't. I was just glad that my mother didn't let dirty dishes pile up in the sink because that's where I liked to play with my World War II–era torpedo-shooting submarine, though for some time I'd been lobbying, without success, for a nuclear-powered upgrade.

15

The Flatbush Diet

You could have asked any Jew in Flatbush and they'd have told you the same thing: Only ignorant goyim (whom I didn't call goyim) used any mayonnaise other than Hellmann's and any ketchup other than Heinz. I knew this was true because every time I ate lunch with the Coogans, Mary Coogan—after digging a dirty plate out of the sink and washing it—would serve me a sandwich, most likely baloney on Wonder Bread slathered with either Kraft mayonnaise or Hunt's ketchup. And these sandwiches were worse than terrible. But I ate them anyway because I was too polite to tell Mary that I didn't like the way they tasted or to ask her why she was feeding me this goyim glop when she could buy the good stuff at the A&P around the corner, like my mother did—my mother who, with near-religious fervor, had indoctrinated me to believe in Hellmann's and Heinz, and to hold all other brands of mayonnaise and ketchup in contempt, especially Kraft and Hunt's.

She also taught me to believe in Campbell's Soup, stocking one entire shelf in our pantry with every flavor in creation: chicken rice, chicken noodle, cream of chicken, cream of

Bobby in Naziland

mushroom, cream of turkey, turkey noodle, turkey rice, turkey vegetable, tomato, tomato rice, split pea, plain vegetable, on and on and on...

Campbell's was the soup she served for lunch, unless she'd made from scratch, using a recipe handed down from her mother, a vat of chicken soup that she called "Jewish Penicillin" because she believed in its powers to cure a cold or the flu. She believed, too, that a regimen of Nabisco Saltine crackers and Coke syrup (which came directly from the Coke machine in the candy store) was the best medicine for the frequent upset stomachs that laid me low when I couldn't face going to school.

My mother also indoctrinated me to believe that kosher (which might as well have been a brand name) meat, especially chicken, was better than non-kosher meat; Cream of Wheat was better than Maypo; H-O was better than Quaker; Bosco was better than Fox's U-Bet; Nestle's Quik was better than Ovaltine (which was just plain weird and Swiss); Skippy was better than Jif; Silvercup was better than Wonder Bread; Carolina was better than Uncle Ben's; Good Humor was better than Bungalow Bar; Bazooka was better than Dubble Bubble; Smith Brothers was better than Vicks (which tasted like the medicine it was supposed to be); My-T Fine puddings were better than Jell-O puddings (though Jell-O gelatin was better than Knox gelatin); and Log Cabin was better than Vermont Maid—though nothing was better than the pure maple syrup somebody once gave my father for Christmas, and which my mother treated as if it were liquid gold, allowing me to put it on my pancakes and French toast only by the teaspoonful, though she acted as if an eyedropper would have been a more appropriate serving implement.

Certain other brands of food, she said, also existed on an elevated plane, without peer, like Aunt Jemima pancake mix,

Philadelphia Cream Cheese, Breakstone's whipped butter, Welch's grape jelly, and Nabisco Devil's Food Squares, which I'd gorge myself on while we waited on the checkout line at the A&P or Waldbaum's.

My mother, however, held no strong opinions about the sickeningly sweet breakfast cereals I asked for every morning, because insidious Mad Men had so thoroughly washed my brain in their brand-name propaganda that my dentist, Doctor Bernstein, should have given them a commission. These cereals included: cartoon-rabbit-endorsed sugarcoated balls called Trix; cartoon-tiger-endorsed Sugar Frosted Flakes; cartoon-bee-endorsed Sugar Pops; superstar-athlete-endorsed Wheaties, the "breakfast of champions," which I'd spike with three heaping tablespoons of white sugar; and all-American-kid-endorsed Kellogg's Corn Flakes, which, when there was no other way to get my morning fix, I'd spike with *four* heaping tablespoons of sugar, because that's how much it took to make those golden flakes of corn sweet enough.

When it came to orange juice, my mother's frugality overpowered her taste buds. But no matter what she said, she couldn't convince me that the off-brand condensed OJ that she always bought at the A&P tasted just as good as Tropicana, which was the brand I'd believed in since I'd tasted it at my grandmother's house. Every time I opened the refrigerator (or "Frigidaire," as everybody called it, though it was actually a Kelvinator), the sight of a pitcher containing water floating on top of thick orange muck appalled me. "It's disgusting!" I'd declare, refusing to drink it, even after a vigorous stirring reconstituted it.

Even more appalling was my mother's insistence that food in the refrigerator *never* spoiled, no matter how long it languished there. It killed her to throw out anything, even if it was covered in mold. "I'll cut off the moldy part!" she'd say. Which is why I never ate or drank anything before sniffing it. And if I detected the slightest hint of disagreeable odor, especially with milk, I'd tell her that it had gone sour and demand she let me throw it out.

"It's not spoiled," she'd say. "It's only the spout that smells bad. Put it back in the Frigidaire. *I'll* drink it."

The milk would then sit in the refrigerator untouched, until a blue-green fungus sprouted from the container, and only then would it vanish, when nobody was looking.

Meat, however, she never allowed to spoil because it was too expensive, and like everybody else (except for "Chiquita" and her son, Eugene Appelberg, the East 18th Street vegetarians) we ate lots of meat, because Americans were supposed to eat meat, especially red meat—it "made you stronger."

Adhering religiously to this dietary dictum, my mother whipped up a meat dish as the main course for every dinner she made, bar none: lamb chops, steak, roast beef, chicken, veal cutlets, duck, turkey, Cornish game hen, meatloaf, hamburgers, cheeseburgers, hot dogs, pork chops, pot roast, corned beef, cabbage stuffed with chop meat, liver, and tongue—a word I took metaphorically until the day in the supermarket that I saw an entire raw tongue wrapped in cellophane and realized that it *was* a cow's tongue, and I refused to eat tongue again, no matter how good it might have tasted. But this revelation didn't stop me from eating most other parts of the cow's body, though not its liver, which looked more repulsive than its tongue and had a flavor I found grotesque, except for when it was served as chopped liver, with lots of Hellmann's mayonnaise.

Say what you will about my mother. She knew how to cook, and she must be given full credit for her near-supernatural ability to transform the most ordinary cut of meat or low-budget piece of fish into something delicious. She would "doctor" a jar of Manischewitz Gefilte Fish using the recipe handed down from her mother, Helen, whose own culinary skills, as far as I knew, were unsurpassed when it came to preparing such Jewish delicacies as the four K's: *kugel*, *kreplach*, *kishka*, and *kasha* (aka noodles, dumplings, sausages, and pasta), the very backbone of the Eastern European diet, the foods that sent family members into spasms of ecstasy whenever she served them. And her great, fluffy matzo balls, the size and consistency of cumulous clouds, were a world unto themselves and a humiliating rejoinder to my other grandmother, Ruth, whose flavorless matzo balls were the size of golf balls and had the consistency of Spaldeens, and whose cooking, my mother said, had driven my father to enlist in the army because he'd heard the food was better there.

What Helen did with an entire kosher chicken or select parts of the bird that less frugal people discarded were magical, too. As the Indians did with the buffalo, she let nothing go to waste, going so far as to suck the marrow from the bones—we all sucked the marrow from the bones—and working wonders with what we called the bird's *pupick*, or bellybutton, which my mother always grabbed before anybody else, proclaiming, "It's my favorite part!"

I'd watched Helen on many occasions transform a gelatinous mass of chicken livers, acquired at the kosher butcher, into sensual mounds of chopped liver, lacing it with gobs of yellow chicken fat (rather than Hellmann's), which she'd rendered herself, and which I liked to spread like butter on white bread. She always kept a jar of chicken fat in the refrigerator to make *gribenes*, a Jewish version of pork rinds: chicken skin deep-fried in chicken fat, resulting in greasy pellets of pure cholesterol, which I ate like popcorn, and which a cardiologist would one day tell me had killed more Jews than Hitler.

My mother, following her mother's instructions to the letter, plunked the store-bought gray lumps of pre-made gefilte fish into a bubbling concoction of spices and vegetables and stewed them for hours, until out from the cauldron came the scrumptious fish-blobs that my father and I devoured, his smothered with horseradish, mine plain.

Sometimes on weekends, she'd whip up a batch of blueberry pancakes or a cheese omelet or cinnamon toast or French toast (often made with challah), occasionally with a serving of ambrosia-like bacon on the side. Though we routinely consumed other pig meats as well—notably pork chops and ham—we also observed Passover. And to make more bearable those eight days of giving up virtually every food I liked to eat, my mother made a mouthwatering *matzoh brei*, *latkes* as light as feathers, and a sponge cake that she then transformed into a strawberry shortcake so delectable it seemed to defeat the very purpose of the holiday—to remember the suffering and deprivations of the Jews who'd wandered in the desert for 40 years.

Her pièces de résistance, however, were her year-round specialties, some of which could be classified as gourmet: chicken cacciatore, veal and eggplant Parmesan, shrimp scampi, spaghetti and meatballs (for which she simmered the meatballs and sauce all day, as if she were Italian), ultra-creamy spinach and potatoes (I'd eat anything with spinach 'cause I liked Popeye), baked apples, which we drowned in heavy cream, and even crêpes suzette, which, she said, were pretty much the same thing as blintzes, except without the filling, and she set them on fire, too, which was the most exciting thing I ever saw her do in the kitchen. And I was ecstatic when she baked her "Depression-era chocolate cake," updating a recipe handed down from my father's mother. Not only did I think this cake was the most luscious food I'd ever tasted, but she let me mix the batter with her Mixmaster, lick the remnants from the beaters and the bowl, and help her make the icing—usually chocolate or vanilla—which she then spread over the cake in an artistic landscape of points, peaks, and swirls that rivaled anything you'd find in the bakery where the Auschwitz lady worked.

16

Modern Art

It should have been her motto: "Money is for necessities," embroidered in needlepoint and hung on the kitchen wall. But after she saw *Dr. Strangelove* the week it opened on Flatbush Avenue, in early 1964, my mother sprang for an unnecessary $1.25 and took me with her to the Loew's Kings so she could see it again.

"You're going to love this movie," she said.

And she was right. I did love *Strangelove*, not so much for the black comedy—which climaxed in Peter Sellers' bravura portrayal of the deranged Nazi scientist Dr. Strangelove, explaining to the president (also Peter Sellers) and the Joint Chiefs of Staff the upside of a global nuclear holocaust—as for the documentary-like shots of the B-52 cockpit, which were more detailed and realistic than anything I'd ever seen before. But what made the day even more memorable was the fact that for those two hours we spent laughing together in the cool darkness of a movie theatre, I enjoyed my mother's company. It was a Saturday afternoon of sheer cinematic pleasure, devoid of all screaming, nagging, threatening, and candy-store talk. Thanks to the talents of the director, *Jewish* Stanley Kubrick, from the Bronx, my mother's much-repressed agreeable side had spontaneously emerged, reminding me that she had one and that she was indeed capable of being a pleasant companion when she wanted to be.

It had been some time since we'd done something quite this much fun. There were nights, long before *Strangelove*, when she'd sit on my bed and read to me, before I went to sleep, from my favorite Dr. Seuss book, *Bartholomew and the Oobleck*, or from *Little Toot*, a picture book about an anthropomorphic tugboat who saves an ocean liner in a storm, or from Poe, or from a Rudyard Kipling book of poems, which included one of her all-time favorites, "Gunga Din," or from my collection of Little Golden Books, like *Nurse Nancy*—I loved that one because my cousin Valerie, a nursing student, had given it to me and because it came with Band Aids decorated with stars and jet fighters, which I liked to wear even if I didn't have a cut.

My mother had also taught me the words to the ever-rousing Army Air Corps song and the Marine Corps hymn. And in 1957, when I was upset because a Vanguard rocket had blown up on the launch pad at Cape Canaveral as America tried to keep up with the Russians and put a satellite into orbit, my mother bought me a model of the rocket, which they'd had in Lamston's, and we sat at the kitchen table as she showed me how to glue the parts together and how to paint the nose cone red, which made me feel better.

A skillful artist, she demonstrated her expertise whenever she could, such as the time I was in the second grade and she helped me make a cover for my school report, "Our Friend the Policeman," showing me how to cut an intricately shaped badge out of an old magazine and paste it on with rubber cement, a substance she considered almost magical because, unlike

Bobby in Naziland

Elmer's Glue, you could rub off with your fingers any excess cement or peel the picture off the page if you hadn't placed it down properly.

Once, when I was in the third grade, she helped me write a report on Pablo Picasso, teaching me about cubism and *The Three Musicians*, and then taking me to the Museum of Modern Art, in Manhattan, so I could see up close that painting's cartoonishly skewed planes. She also showed me *Baboon and Young*, Picasso's metal sculpture of a monkey carrying its baby, made of *objets trouvés*, a term I learned that day. He'd used a toy car for the baboon's head and a frying pan for its ass, the handle serving as its tail. I knew as I gazed upon the sculpture that I was looking at genius, though that wasn't the word that came to mind then—I simply couldn't imagine seeing an old skillet lying in a pile of junk and thinking, yes, that could be a baboon's ass and tail.

I was even more taken by Jackson Pollock's insane swirling splatters that filled enormous canvases covering entire walls in the silent, sterile rooms, the paintings' manic energy exciting me as I stood there staring at them and thinking that if I wanted to, I could stand on top of a ladder and splash paint all over a pristine white surface. Anybody could do it. It was easy!

Later that day, as we were leaving the museum, my mother told me that she'd wanted to be an artist when she was younger—that's what she'd wanted to do as a career. She knew that she had some talent, a talent that now mostly manifested itself in the posters she made for the PTA. But she also knew that she didn't have the drive and the willpower required to survive being rejected over and over again. She said that though her artistic dreams had died long before she'd gotten married, she continued to love art and artists, books and authors, but believed that creative endeavors were not something that real people—like her, like me, and like anybody else we knew (such as her uncle Jacob, whose musical ambitions had cost him his right hand)—did professionally. Which is why, when I told her that I wanted to be a writer, she could barely contain her rage as she said to me, "Do you have any idea how hard it is to make a living doing that?"

I didn't have a clue, and I said, "No. How hard is it?"

She just looked at me, shaking her head, as if I'd said something stupid.

I had no idea why she was so angry. I hadn't *done* anything.

17

A World of Grudge

It could have been nothing more than a minor snub—a non-invitation to a distant cousin's bar mitzvah in Jerusalem that they wouldn't have gone to even if they'd been invited. Or it could have been a cosmic cataclysm like the Holocaust. The scale of the offense was irrelevant. What was important was that a grudge-worthy transgression had been committed, and now the person who was the victim of that transgression, along with his or her closest relatives, was going to bear that grudge for decades... possibly for all eternity, be it against a second cousin or the Third Reich. And I'm not just talking about my parents—though they could carry a grudge as well as any Hatfield or McCoy. I'm talking about virtually *everybody* on both sides of the family. They were all world-class grudge bearers, and they all dreamed of the day that they'd be able to serve their revenge at any temperature.

There were so many free-floating grudges in circulation, at times it seemed as if everybody in the family despised everybody else in the family (if not the world). Sometimes when a person my parents hated died, they'd barely acknowledge it to each other, much less to me (they'd rarely tell me when *anybody* had died), because metaphorically speaking, this hated person was already dead to them, and now that he or she was dead for real, it didn't make much difference.

Of course, when these despicable people still walked the earth, the only thing my parents ever told me about them was how much they hated them, though they rarely explained why. So I knew little about these relatives (at least they were usually relatives), except for what I'd been able to observe firsthand when the family gathered for a bar mitzvah or wedding that we *were* invited to and one side ignored the other side while we were all in the same room, sometimes sitting at the same table.

To this day, aside from their names, I don't know who a dozen or so relatives were, or why my parents hated them so much that I never got to meet them when they were alive and wasn't told when they'd died—always for my own good, my parents would later say, always because they didn't want to upset me with things that I didn't have a need to know... until 10 or 20 or even 50 years later, when I'd finally find out about them on my own.

They did, however, tell me about one estranged relative, my father's "rich" cousin Abe. Right before my father had gone into the candy store business with my grandfather, he was in the insurance business with Abe, and Abe had swindled him out of a "small fortune." But when my parents spoke of this crime, as they often did (though always in the vaguest terms and the darkest, most poisonous whispers), they never said *how* Abe had swindled my father or how much a small fortune was. Anytime I asked my mother about it, she said the same thing: "Don't ever mention Abe to your father. If it weren't for Abe we'd have been rich."

I knew that wasn't true. I knew that people who became

rich didn't spend their lives looking back in regret at mistakes they'd made in the distant past or at things that somebody had once done to them. Rich people made money no matter what happened—because they looked forward, they moved on. That much I'd learned from watching an episode of *The Real McCoys*, in which Grandpa McCoy—Walter Brennan—lost all his money and immediately started scheming to make more money with some kind of crazy idea. Grandpa McCoy remained completely positive, even excited, in the face of financial ruin. He saw his situation as a challenge. He knew he was going to make more money somehow, and he was going to start making it *now*. Making money for him was a game, not an ordeal. And he didn't blame any Hatfields, either.

But I wasn't a real McCoy, was I? I was a real Rosen, which felt like more than enough reality to handle on most days.

One family exception: My uncle Herb's wife, Barbara, held no grudges against anybody, and she'd made it her business for decades to meet every family member that she could. Many times, over the years, she'd start telling me about a long-dead relative whom my parents had despised and I'd never met. One night during dinner she brought up a great-uncle, and I dimly recalled—or thought I did—the time, five decades earlier, that I'd last heard somebody utter this person's name, Harry. My mother had whispered it to my father, as a question, and then, when he was out of earshot, told me, "Your father's upset today. Somebody he knew died."

"Who?"

"Nobody you know."

Now, 45 years after the fact, over a couple of burgers in a restaurant, I was hearing from my aunt, in her convoluted way, that this person was my father's uncle and that my great-uncle Harry had two sons, a little younger than my father, one of whom, Arthur, had committed suicide, though Barbara wasn't sure when.

I didn't know my grandfather *had* a brother. And I was left reeling from the double shock of learning about three blood relatives I never knew existed—even though we'd all lived in Brooklyn—and the fact that one of them had killed himself.

Was it Harry's death my mother was whispering about to my father on that almost forgotten day in 1962? Or was it Arthur's?

My aunt then told me that my great-uncle Harry's other son, Michael, was a well-to-do photographer specializing in "radical sexuality," as he called it, and living in San Francisco. "He's a regular Robert Mapplethorpe," she said.

That was the third shock of the meal: the existence of a *living* blood relative, well known in certain avant-garde circles, who shares my last name and whom nobody had ever mentioned to me before—even though our paths could have crossed during my own career in erotic magazines.

"Why did my father hate these people so much?" I asked my aunt.

The hatred, Barbara explained, dated back to when my grandfather Julius—or "Julie," as she called him—was stricken with multiple sclerosis (I'd always been told it was Lou Gehrig's disease) and my grandmother Ruth thought that her in-laws were treating Julius badly, the final rupture having something to do with their refusal to drive him to a doctor's appointment. So my grandmother—and her three sons—stopped talking to them. Forever. It wasn't much of an explanation, but it was better than anything I'd ever heard before.

Other significant information my grandmother never told

Bobby in Naziland

anybody about, taking it with her to the grave. It wasn't until after Ruth died, at age 95—an event that no one mentioned to my father until after the funeral because of an ongoing feud he was having with his two brothers—that one of my uncles discovered some mysterious "papers" which indicated that Ruth had been "adopted" after both her parents had died, though it wasn't clear if she was legally adopted or just taken in by relatives. This meant that the woman my father and his brothers thought was Ruth's mother was really her aunt. For whatever reason, Ruth had chosen not to share this information with her three sons. And though she said she was born in America, most of her relatives—like my mother—thought she had been born in Russia or Poland and just didn't want people to know she was an immigrant, because being an immigrant was considered "lower class" (in a "class-free" society). As it turned out, Ruth *was* born in New York City, though I didn't find this out until long after she was dead, my father was dead, and my ever-industrious non-grudge-carrying aunt Barbara tracked down the information on Ancestry.com. (When I was a kid, I knew this much about my grandmother: When her husband, Julius, became ill, she took care of him until he died, and she never went out with another man for the rest of her life. Once, when I was about five, while sleeping over at her house, I heard her talking in her sleep to my dead grandfather, and I refused to ever sleep over there again because I thought it was creepy.)

There were also plenty of things my grandmother didn't know about me, because I never told her anything, like what I did for a living. Apparently nobody else did, either, for good reason: Ruth believed that anyone who wasn't a doctor, a lawyer, or a scientist was a failure—like my father, the soda jerk—and in her eyes, being a writer was somewhat lower-class than working in a candy store. I presume she presumed that I did nothing respectable, or close to nothing, which for too long a time was pretty close to the truth.

Even before I figured out, when I was about 11, that almost nothing my parents had told me about the family was completely true, I must have unconsciously sensed an enormous gap between their words and reality, and it left me hungry for the truth—about anything.

I just didn't know where to look for it, and before discovering a world of truth about the Nazis in *The Rise and Fall of the Third Reich*, it never occurred to me that I might find it in books.

The books I was forced to read in school, like *Fun with Dick and Jane*, which was set in a sterilized suburban world that never existed, at least on Planet Earth, contained little resembling truth. Nor was any to be found in *Tom Swift* and *The Hardy Boys*, though, unlike *Dick and Jane*, they were fun to read. And there was certainly no truth in most of the junk I watched on TV, like the saccharine *Romper Room* with its goody-two-shoes third-graders, who bored me to death, and *The Shari Lewis Show* with that stupid hand-puppet Lamb Chop. Even more ridiculous were those "public service" announcements featuring Nikita Khrushchev, the premier of the Soviet Union, banging his shoe on a table and shouting, "We will bury you!" These propaganda spots, designed to make little kids hate Communism, ran on the Saturday morning cartoon shows. At least there was some truth in those Warner Brothers cartoons—conveyed by Daffy Duck, the Roadrunner, and especially Bugs Bunny (born in Flatbush, *on my birthday*, July 27, 1940, in a rabbit warren under Ebbets Field!), who taught me that being smart and clever or just saying the right words at the right time was the best way to get out of trouble; and Elmer Fudd, Porky Pig, Wile E. Coyote, and Yosemite Sam, who taught me that people who shot off their big guns and big mouths were nothing but fools and bullies. But I didn't recognize it as truth because I didn't yet understand that the easiest way to make somebody laugh is to tell the truth.

Since nobody had ever told me the truth about sex, I had to figure out what I could on my own, not only from Jeffrey Abromovitz (who, as I've noted, was only vaguely aware of the existence of the vagina) and whatever foul-mouthed juvenile delinquents I'd overhear spouting off about "fucking" neighborhood "*hooahs*," like Aileen Murphy, and how they put their dicks in the "*hooahs*'" mouths (which sounded like a strange thing to do), but from my parents' marriage manual, *The Art of Love*, a thin blue volume that materialized one day in the bookcase, right next to *The Life and Times of the Shmoo*, by Al Capp.

This manual, I soon realized, contained just as much truth as *The Rise and Fall of the Third Reich*, and it was better pornography, too, because it was *real* pornography—erotica—and I assume my parents left it there to alleviate themselves of the responsibility of having to tell me the truth about sex.

So, it's not as if they were opposed to truth. Quite the opposite. My parents were fine with the truth, as long as it had nothing to do with them or the family, and as long as they didn't have to be the ones to tell me the truth, except for maybe the truth about the Holocaust, which was, admittedly, a large chunk of truth to digest.

18

Something Different Happened

If she wasn't listening to soap operas like *Young Doctor Malone* or *The Guiding Light* on the kitchen radio as she washed dishes or cooked up a cauldron of her kosher-chicken soup, then my mother was listening to William B. Williams' *Make Believe Ballroom*, on WNEW-AM, "eleven-three-oh on your dial." The sounds of the Big Band Era filled the room with The Harry James Orchestra, or with Dinah Shore, Bing Crosby, or Rosemary Clooney. It was all mush to my ears, though I did like it when Peggy Lee belted out "Hey! Look Me Over" or Ella Fitzgerald sang "From This Moment On" or Dean Martin (*He drinks but what do you expect from a goy?*) crooned "Volare." Williams was always playing Frank Sinatra, too. He called Sinatra "Francis Albert," and my mother called him a "*mensch*" because when my father had taken her to a Dodgers Game at Ebbets Field in the summer of 1948, Sinatra (a great baseball fan who'd one day record a song about the Brooklyn Dodgers, "There Used to Be a Ballpark") was sitting a few rows in front of them and graciously signed her program. I liked Sinatra's "You Make Me Feel So Young" because unlike so much of the other stuff Williams played, it had a bouncy beat.

Bobby in Naziland

And I *really* liked "High Hopes," Sinatra's inspirational song about the ant who moved the rubber tree plant, because it made me feel good every time I heard it. But that was about it.

I was, however, nuts about *South Pacific*, a Broadway musical my father had taken my mother to see before I was born—one of the many things they did back then that they didn't do anymore because doing things cost money. So impressed were they with the show, they bought the original-cast recording, a portfolio of 78s, one song on each side of each disc. I played *South Pacific* more than they did, from beginning to end, because I thought that was how you were supposed to do it. I played that album so much I knew most of the words by heart. And though I was puzzled by the description in "A Cockeyed Optimist" of the "bright canary yellow" sky, because I'd never seen a sky that was any shade of yellow, I thought "There Is Nothing Like a Dame" was one of the two best songs I'd ever heard, the complexity of its lyrics and the intricate, unexpected rhymes and exuberant melodies filling my head with exotic visions of palm trees and tropical beaches.

The always stirring "This Is the Army, Mr. Jones" was my other favorite song. But except for that and one other tune, "Oh, How I Hate to Get Up in the Morning," the show album *This Is the Army* didn't come close to *South Pacific*. Still, in the sixth grade, I chose to write a report about the composer, *Jewish* Irving Berlin, and my mother helped me draw a piano keyboard in India ink for the cover. Our teacher, Mr. Yanklowitz, then asked everybody to bring in an album by the composer they'd written about. But Yanklowitz wouldn't play *This Is the Army* because, as he told me privately after class, "Nobody wants to hear this kind of music."

I didn't tell him that he didn't know what he was talking about and that I thought the music was better than any of the 33⅓ rpm long-playing record albums from current Broadway shows like *Bye Bye Birdie* and *The Sound of Music*, and movies like *West Side Story*, that my classmates had brought in.

Yanklowitz didn't understand, and neither did I, that I'd brought in *This Is the Army* because I was living in a time warp, that a wall of pure energy, a Great Psychic Wall, had been holding time (as well as most Negros and Puerto Ricans) at bay throughout the neighborhood, especially on East 17ᵗʰ Street.

It made little difference if in the real world it was 1956 or 1960 or even 1963. In Fortress Flatbush, time, primarily when it came to music and other aspects of what was not yet commonly known as "pop culture," had stopped somewhere in the mid-to-late 1940s, and only in the limited upscale areas where many of my classmates lived had it progressed into the 1950s and in some cases beyond, allowing them access to popular Broadway and movie musicals and the advanced technology of the LPs they were recorded on.

The Wall had kept the influence of Elvis, along with the rest of rock 'n' roll, to a bare minimum, though Bill Haley & His Comets had found their way to me. My uncle Paul had given me a 45 of "Dim Dim the Lights" so he could listen to it on my phonograph; his mother wouldn't let him play records in the house. The song was OK, I thought, but I still liked "There Is Nothing Like a Dame" more.

And The Wall had kept out folk music, too, including the likes of that emerging *Jewish* genius Bob Dylan, who might have gotten through if he'd kept his real name, Robert Zimmerman. In fact the only "folk singer" who'd breached The Wall wasn't even a folk singer. He was *Jewish* Allan Sherman and he'd recorded an album of parody songs, *My Son the Folk Singer*, which was the first LP my parents ever bought.

That's because comedy was a different story, and the old-school Jewish comedians, like Buddy Hackett, from Borough Park—*"He went to high school with your father!"*—Shecky Greene, Alan King, Milton Berle, and Mel Brooks vied with each other for the title of World's Funniest Jew. These people were not only welcomed into Fortress Flatbush; they were worshipped like comedic gods when they appeared on the great shrine of *The Ed Sullivan Show*... except for Lenny Bruce, a *Jewish junkie*, for God's sake, the lowest form of life, bar none; and Woody Allen, a nebbishy *Jewish* embarrassment from the adjacent Midwood neighborhood. They never made it over The Wall, and their names remained unspoken.

Vaughn Meader was different, too, because he was one of a select group of goyim who'd made it over The Wall. The second LP my parents bought was his Kennedy-lampooning comedy album, *The First Family*, and they played it (along with *My Son the Folk Singer*) every time somebody came to visit, with the bit about Jackie, in her overly breathy voice, leading White House visitors past the "Nixon dumbwaiter" always provoking the most laughter. Also any number of harmless singing goyim, like Andy Williams, Perry Como, and Pat Boone, had penetrated via radio and TV, and even the *schvartze* Nat King Cole had made it through, though only God knows how Chubby Checker and his "Twist"—a dance I taught myself after I saw it on TV, and which I performed on request for my baby sitter, Eloise—had breeched Fortress Flatbush and infected my very household.

Then, one Friday afternoon in November, The Wall began to crumble. I was in school when it happened, because that's where you're supposed to be when you're 11 years old, and I was deep into a state of unrelenting boredom, my seventh year of unrelenting PS 249 boredom... boredom that I feared would never end.

The day went cinematic around 1:30, when the teacher from the adjoining classroom opened the door to our classroom and motioned for Mr. Yanklowitz to come out into the hall, an odd occurrence in itself. I could see the two of them, just outside the door, talking, and then Yanklowitz stepped back into the room, and, miracle of miracles, he dismissed the class, told us to go home, and said that our parents would explain what had happened.

There was stunned silence, and then the sound of chairs scraping against the floor, followed by a stampede of feet towards the coat closet in the back of the room, and the excited chatter of kids getting out of school an hour and a half early on a Friday afternoon because *something different had happened*, and our parents would tell us about it when we got home.

Out on Marlborough Road there was another strange sight: a dozen cars lined up like a funeral cortege, mothers of kids I knew sitting behind the wheel, waiting for them. Some of the mothers were weeping as they listened to their radios, the news pouring out through open car windows: *President Kennedy died this afternoon, in Dallas...*

He'd been shot!

A pervasive sense of strangeness surrounded me as I walked alone towards Caton Avenue, past the decrepit and eerily silent rooming house on the corner. I was thinking about the poster hanging on my bedroom wall, a portrait of JFK and Jackie that my uncle Herb, my father's brother, had given to me as a birthday present.

Caton Avenue, too, was oddly quiet for this time of day, and the Parade Grounds were completely deserted. I couldn't see a single soul anywhere on the vast scruffy expanse of baseball diamonds and football fields.

Bobby in Naziland

That was when Jeffrey Abromovitz came up behind me and, motioning towards the Parade Grounds, asked, "You want to play football?"

I immediately understood what Abromovitz was getting at: If we got there fast, we'd have an opportunity that might never come again. Rather than play on whatever patch of dirt or grass was available, which we normally did at the Parade Grounds when we played football—the game the Kennedy clan so famously played at their Hyannis Port compound (so famously lampooned on *The First Family* album)—we could have an entire football field to ourselves, goal posts included, and we'd be able to practice kicking field goals, a skill my father had told me would make me rich if I could master it.

When I got home, I found my mother sitting on the couch, already transfixed by the TV, Jerrold in her lap sucking on his bottle. She said nothing about any dead presidents when I walked in. I glanced at the TV. A man was reading the news: *Kennedy... Kennedy... Kennedy...* And I thought about the time in third grade, on the eve of the 1960 election, when Mrs. Feinstein had polled the class, and Kennedy had gotten *100 percent* of the votes. It was unanimous—even eight-year-olds were on to Nixon.

I went to my room to take off my white shirt, red tie, and black pants—my Friday-school-assembly clothes—and change into a pair of dungarees (as they were called at the time), Keds (better than PF Flyers), and a sweatshirt, vaguely conscious of the poster on the wall, JFK's and Jackie's eyes following me around my bedroom.

I grabbed my football, and again poking my head into the living room (and neglecting to mention I was meeting Abromovitz), I told my mother, "I'm going to the park."

"Don't stay out too late," she said, not taking her eyes off the TV.

Abromovitz was the only other person in the Parade Grounds, a lone figure leaning against a goal post. I tossed him a perfect spiral; about a month or two earlier my hand had at last grown large enough to grip the ball properly. He caught it cleanly.

So there we were, Abromovitz and me, bathed in sparkling autumn sunlight, on an empty gridiron in an empty park, the world having gone silent around us, as we took turns trying to kick field goals. And even though I was a decent kicker, especially for my age, capable of getting off the occasional booming punt, I discovered on November 22, 1963, that place-kicking with a holder was something completely different, even from 10 yards out with nobody rushing you.

The best either of us could do was hit the crossbar.

The voice, sharp and accusatory, startled me: "How can you be out playing on a day like this?"

I turned around. An old man I'd never seen before had snuck up behind us. He was wearing a black overcoat, even though it was unseasonably warm, probably about 60 degrees. "Don't you know the president's been assassinated?" he said.

It was the first time I'd heard somebody call what happened "assassinated," and I thought it was an interesting word.

"Mind your own business, mister," I told him, surprising myself with a tone far snottier than I intended it to be.

I then returned to what I was doing and shagged another field-goal attempt as the man, shaking his head, walked towards Caton Avenue, looking back only once to see that his words had had no effect upon us whatsoever.

We soon gave up on field goals and spent the rest of the afternoon taking turns playing quarterback and running square outs, buttonhooks, and post patterns. By the time dusk fell, we were exhausted, and I walked home to take my place in front of the TV with the rest of America, thus joining the all-Kennedy-all-the-time marathon, *The Dead President Show*, a constant stream of ghost-shadowed images of a motorcade, the president and Jackie in an open car, waving to the crowd, and then a coffin, flags, mourners, a show that would last for four interminable days during which, by day two, I longed to see anything else, longed for sitcomic relief—a half-hour of *My Favorite Martian* to break the monotony, or just a few minutes of *The Twilight Zone* or *The Outer Limits* or *The Fugitive* or *McHale's Navy* or even *Bonanza*... anything!

"I'm sick of this," I told my mother on day four, the day of the funeral, which we'd gone to watch at my grandmother Helen's house. "It's all the same."

"It's not all the same," she said, directing my attention to the TV, where JFK Jr., little John-John, on his third birthday—a year older than my blissfully oblivious baby brother, Jerrold, who might have been Jacqueline—stood alongside his mother, his sister, Caroline, and his uncle Robert and saluted his father's flag-draped coffin as seven white horses pulled it through the streets of Washington.

And even I had to admit, yes, this *was* different—the spectacle of a traumatized family, so different from my own, holding it together before the entire world.

Helen was giving the TV her full attention, too. When it came to JFK, she was always willing to ignore the fact that he was a goy *and* a Catholic and that his father, as she and so many others believed, was an Irish bootlegger who *knew* what he was doing. Born on the shtetl, ironically on St. Patrick's Day, she thought all goyim were good-for-nothing drunkards at best, an opinion invariably confirmed on her birthday when it looked as if they were celebrating her entrance into the world with a booze-soaked bacchanal on Fifth Avenue. The exception was Kennedy, who she thought was so handsome, his looks transcended his goyishness. She'd seen him up close one afternoon, in 1960, when she'd gotten off the subway on Avenue U, in Brooklyn, and there he was, 10 feet away, up on a platform, giving a campaign speech. She practically swooned.

"He was *so* good-looking," she said. "And his hair was red, not the way it looks in pictures."

And then he went and got his matinee-idol head blown off, and we all saw it on TV—blood and brains in black-and-white, but blood and brains just the same—and we read in the newspapers about his stunned expression as the first bullet hit, and bits of bone and brain, the president's brain, splattered all over Jackie, sitting next to him in that open limousine rolling down a Dallas street. And then we saw the blood and brains in color in *Life* magazine and elsewhere, on Jackie's "pink Chanel suit"... Jackie, who wore that blood-and-brain-stained pink dress all day long so we could all "see what they did to him." And then we saw Oswald, the assassin, murdered live on TV before they had a chance to stick Kennedy in the ground—a bullet tearing through his guts, the look of agony on his face, as iconic as the blood and brains on Jackie's dress.

We behind the great crumbling Wall of Fortress Flatbush saw it all—live, recorded, in black-and-white, in color—and boy, was it ever different, a new kind of information seeping through in real time, which could no longer be held at bay, and which I didn't like very much now that it was slowly filling my world.

For one thing, that portrait of JFK and Jackie hanging on my bedroom wall had to go—it freaked me out to look at it, especially at night when I was trying to fall asleep. JFK's eyes would stare

Bobby in Naziland

at me, and I kept seeing him as a corpse with its head blown off, lying on an autopsy slab, like when I was younger and kept seeing Robert Rosenberg on the night of his parents' execution.

But that didn't stop me from listening to *The First Family* album—not immediately after the assassination, but soon after they'd buried Kennedy at Arlington. I did it secretly, when nobody else was home, because I knew I wasn't supposed to be listening to it—just as I knew years earlier that I wasn't supposed to be reading *The Rise and Fall of the Third Reich*. I thought the album was still funny, but in a different way than it had been a few weeks earlier. It was an entirely new kind of funny, a macabre and unintentional funny that would soon manifest itself, intentionally, in *Dr. Strangelove*.

Amidst the weekly blizzards and repeated school closings of that grim winter of 1963 and '64, it seemed that every magazine that went on sale in my father's candy store—*Life*, *Look*, *Time*, *Newsweek*, *The Saturday Evening Post*, and even *Playboy*—had something about the Kennedy assassination on the cover. There was no getting away from it, and even I understood how profoundly everything had changed, how overnight the double murder of the movie-star president and then his killer, a scrawny creep named Lee Harvey Oswald (*Life* magazine would soon publish his diaries), had shrouded America in a fog of sadness, making it seem like one of those coup-prone Central American countries Mr. Yanklowitz had told us about, a banana republic now run by that ugly big-eared son-of-a-bitch Texan, LBJ. (One year later, on an October afternoon, a Secret Service agent turned down my father's offer to send an egg cream out to Johnson as he rode down Church Avenue in an open limousine with Bobby Kennedy. A moment later, the limo was mobbed by the waiting crowd on the corner of East 17th Street, allowing me to reach up and shake the president's hand, which prompted another Secret Service agent to deliver a painful karate chop to my forearm.)

As if we weren't thinking enough about Kennedy on our own, they made us think about him in school, too.

"Your homework assignment," said Yanklowitz one January day, "is to write a report about how we can honor President Kennedy. And don't say 'Rename Marlborough Road Kennedy Road.' Be original."

The traditional thing to do with a dead president, I wrote in my "Honoring Kennedy" report, was to put his face on money. About half the class had the same idea.

Something different was in the air when February came, and you didn't have to listen to rock 'n' roll radio, on WMCA, to know about it. William B. Williams mentioned it on *The Make Believe Ballroom*; my father's candy store cronies commented on it as they scanned the newspapers; and my classmates, especially the girls, who'd never breathed a word to me about Elvis, were suddenly all aflutter, saying things like, "Don't you think they're gorgeous?"

They were coming to New York and they were going to be on TV.

Like everybody else I'd heard the music. It was unavoidable. It had burst through The Wall, just as Kennedy had, little snippets of it pouring from TV sets when you listened to the news, and from transistor radios, both my own and the ones teenagers, boys and girls alike, held in their hands as they walked down Church Avenue, the sounds carrying both an electrifying energy and, it seemed, yet another new kind of information.

Bobby in Naziland

I already knew some of the songs by name, like "I Wanna Hold Your Hand," and a lot of the words, too, at least the ones that I could understand—they didn't sing clearly, like Rosemary Clooney and Frank Sinatra did.

They touched down at JFK, formerly Idlewild, the airport rechristened in December to honor the dead president. Four young men with long hair, whom I could not yet differentiate, emerged from a Pan Am jet as the throngs of greeters screamed their ecstatic welcome. I watched it on TV again and again, another loop, like Maris's 61st home run—but this time the soundtrack was those amazing songs, played over and over on every station.

The energy surged all the way into Brighton Hall, infecting at least one neighbor, Stephanie Coogan, who lived downstairs with her ever-expanding brood of siblings. She was 14, the perfect age to become a Beatlemaniac, and as I was walking out of the building that Friday afternoon, she grabbed my arm.

"I've got a phone number for the Beatles!" she said, pressing a scrap of paper into my hand. "Here, you can have this. You can call them at the hotel and they'll talk to you."

I had no doubt this was true. Why wouldn't it be? I went around the corner to the candy store so I could call them privately, from the phone booth. Dropping a dime in the slot, I dialed the number. The phone rang, probably the phone at the front desk of the Plaza Hotel, where they were staying, though I was sure it was ringing in the Beatles' room, just as I was sure they were all in the same room, and that one of them was about to answer. Then somebody picked up the phone, but I got scared and hung up. What would I say to a Beatle? I had no idea. I didn't even know their names.

Seventy-eight days after the assassination, Sunday, February 9, at 8 p.m., I sat down in front of our TV, on the threadbare living room carpet. My mother, on the couch to my right, was still working on the *Times* crossword puzzle. My father, who'd worked the day shift, was behind me in the club chair, flipping through the main section of the paper. And my brother, in the other room, was already sound asleep. Though I was unaware that 73 million other Americans had positioned themselves in a similar fashion, in their own living rooms, I did have an inkling that *The Dead President Show* might finally be over and something much more alive was about to begin transmission.

But first there appeared the MC, Ed Sullivan, with the same pasty face I'd been looking at for as long as I could remember, every week at this very same time, the same oily, swept-back hair, a little mound of it front and center, the same herky-jerky movements. And, yes, he spoke with that voice every impressionist knew how to imitate, sometimes on this very show: *Right right here on our stage...* And then there was a magician doing card tricks, followed by an Anacin commercial.

At 8:12, according to the clock on the end table, Sullivan, seeming like a self-parody, began his introduction for "the youngsters from Liverpool" who will "twice entertain you." The shrieking commenced on cue, and there they were, in black-and-white, four musicians with their crazy haircuts, in neckties and strange-looking sport jackets. Three of them had guitars, the drummer was mounted on a platform behind them, and the whole group was surrounded by giant arrows pointing their way, as if we wouldn't have noticed them otherwise. The sound roaring out of the TV was an explosion of pure joy. I knew the first song, "All My Loving," and despite the girls in the audience screaming their heads off, practically drowning out the music, my parents and I took it all in quietly, just as we'd have watched any other *Ed Sullivan Show*.

My mother knew the second song, "Till There Was You."

"It's from *The Music Man*," she said helpfully.

Then they sang another song I knew, possibly my favorite, "She Loves You."

"'Yeah, yeah, yeah'?" my father inquired, unhelpfully.

"Yeah," I said.

"Did you know their manager's Jewish?" my mother asked me.

"No."

"His name's *Epstein*."

The Beatles returned to finish the show with "I Saw Her Standing There," as I later learned it was called, and that other song I liked and knew a lot of the words to, "I Want to Hold Your Hand."

Then, still unaware that the 1940s had once and for all come to an end in my apartment as well as in most other homes on the wrong side of East 17th Street, and that the *present* had come rushing in like fresh air, as if filling a vacuum, I saw that it was time to switch to Channel 4, for *Bonanza*.

I did know one thing, however: Whatever it was I'd just heard, I wanted more.

The following day, with three dollar bills in my pocket, the fruits of three hours of candy store work, I went to Lamston's, the five-and-dime next door to the candy store. I didn't have to look hard for what I wanted. There were two binfuls of two different record albums, right up front, greeting me as I walked in.

The album on the left had a red cover with a couple of snapshots of the Beatles, and it featured my favorite song, "She

Loves You." But I'd never heard any of the other songs listed on the back. And though the interviews interspersed with these songs might be interesting, I was pretty sure I'd only want to listen to them once. I put the record back in the bin.

The other album was nothing but music, including "I Want to Hold Your Hand" and "All My Loving," the two songs I liked almost as much as "She Loves You," and that song from *The Music Man* that my mother liked and that I didn't think was half-bad. The cover photo, too, appealed to me in a way I couldn't quite explain. Set against a black background were four chalk-white faces topped with that astoundingly long dark hair, a stark contrast to my own crew cut. Three of the faces were placed across the top, the fourth below and to the right. But it was the writing on the back cover that made an even deeper impression. This was not the kind of information they had on *South Pacific* or *This Is the Army*, and it certainly wasn't the sort of thing I'd ever read in a book. These liner notes, which I didn't know were called "liner notes," described the insane dimensions of Beatlemania, discussed the band's "pudding basin haircuts that date back to ancient England" and their collarless jackets, and distinguished one Beatle from the other by noting which instruments they played (What's a mouth organ? What are claves?), who wrote which song, and who sang which song. Below this was a photo that put names to those faces on the front cover: Paul McCartney, George Harrison, Ringo Starr, and John Lennon... Lennon, who, unbeknownst to me, had his own ideas about Nazis and Jews, and who not that long ago had played in Hamburg strip joints for the very "Nazis" who'd carpet-bombed his beloved Liverpool the day he was born, shouting "*Sieg heil!*" at them between songs and somehow making them laugh. Lennon, who'd famously call his manager, Brian Epstein, a "queer Jew" (though not in these or any other liner notes); who'd do more than any other Beatle to tear down the Psychic Wall of Flatbush; and whose *assassination* 17 years later would extinguish whatever flickering embers still remained of "the 60s," the decade that, unbeknownst to anybody, had truly been born a mere 79 days earlier, when the gunshots rang out in Dallas.

It was a couple of sentences in small type on the bottom that clinched the deal. I look at those words now, on the antique LP I still have, the cover worn but the record itself in pristine condition, indicating more than a half-century of tender loving care: "This monographic microgroove recording is playable on monographic and stereo phonographs. It cannot become obsolete."

Both albums were priced at three dollars, and though I badly wanted "She Loves You," I bought *Meet the Beatles* instead of the schlocky-looking one-off, aware that for the first time in my life, I possessed music I could call my own.

At home, I played both sides of the album, from beginning to end, and I knew I'd made the right decision. There were no songs on it I didn't like, which was not the case with *South Pacific* or *This Is the Army*. Then I began playing the record nonstop, day after day. When "Till There Was You" (third song, side two) came on, my mother would often stand in the door of my room and listen. I played *Meet the Beatles* so much, I memorized all the lyrics. I found myself singing quietly in the shower, spontaneously making up my own parody lyrics to Beatles melodies: "Oh yeah, I'll tell you something/There's a Beatle on your grass/And I'll tell you something/those Beatles do have class..." I didn't know why I was doing this. I'd never done anything like that before.

I took the album to Barry Gardner's house—I finally had something that he didn't have—and, half-expecting/half-hoping that the girls who lived in neighboring apartments would climb down the fire escape and come in through the windows to listen to the Beatles with us, we played the LP, beginning to end, on his father's state-of-the-art hi-fi, studying the album cover front and back as we listened, opening ourselves to the information the four musicians had brought to us from across the ocean, trying to decode what they were transmitting, unconsciously sensing new possibilities that we couldn't express, yet somehow knowing that we were being swept along to who knows where on the winds of change.

19

A Head Full of Holocaust

But not even the Beatles could save me from myself, not in 1964 anyway. In the autumn of that year, as the first anniversary of the Kennedy assassination approached—again filling the air with ceaseless chatter of bullets, blood, and brains, of a lone gunman and of conspiracies, reminding us of what we were not permitted to ever forget—I closed the door to my bedroom and, bracing myself against the wall, began to contemplate smashing my right shoulder with the ball-peen hammer I was holding in my left hand. I didn't know why, exactly, I wanted to do this. It just seemed like a good idea, one that I couldn't express in words.

Some 50 years later, it doesn't take Sigmund Freud to see that I was one *meshuggener* kid with a head full of Holocaust, executions, and assassinations, engulfed in a morass of hatred, horror, and guilt. Like the concentration-camp survivor in the film *The Pawnbroker* (played by Rod Steiger), who impales his hand on a spike, I must have understood in a primal way that searing physical pain can feel like pleasure for at least a few moments as it obliterates the perpetual throb of emotional pain.

But all I knew as I stood against the wall was that for as long as I could remember, I'd felt fucked up most of the time, I didn't like feeling that way, and I wanted to do something about it.

Even if I could have put into words a fraction of what was really going on in my head, I wouldn't have. I'd never heard anybody *complain* about the Holocaust, not even the people who'd survived it—especially the people who'd survived it. If the Nazis had subjected you to their abominations, then you lived with it quietly, like my friend Daniel Silver's mother, Liba, did. In other words, if I'd told my mother and father, "The Holocaust and all this assassination business is making me feel very upset," or words to that effect, it would have been so out of character, they'd have probably burst out laughing. Or my mother would have said, "Just don't think about the Holocaust and assassinations. Now go do your homework or you'll never get into college. You're the only one in your class who didn't make the SP. You could have skipped the eighth grade."

Yes, I'd screwed up the math on the test that would have put me in the accelerated program. Which is another reason I thought that self-mutilation with a hammer might be the answer to my problem. I knew on some instinctive level that if I beat the shit out of myself with a blunt instrument, it just might make me feel better.

The idea had been festering in my brain since the day I saw the picture in the family photo album of my mother in her famous cast. I must have heard the story a thousand times about how, in her younger days, when she used to go horseback riding—a hobby underwritten by my grandfather's lofty supermarket-manager salary—she'd shattered her shoulder when she was thrown from a horse, and following surgical reconstruction, her torso and upper arm were encased in an enormous cast, soon covered in autographs, with her arm sticking out at a 45-degree angle.

That photo took on a near-religious significance to me, like the holy cards my downstairs neighbor James Coogan Jr. used for bookmarks in his Bible and catechism, and at some point—probably in the second grade—I got it into my head that I, too, wanted to break a bone and be sheathed in a great cast, just like my mother. What better way, I thought, to get a little attention and bring a touch of glamour to my distinctly drab and under-appreciated life?

The opportunity to accomplish this presented itself in seventh grade, at Ditmas, my new school. Because I, again, lived on the wrong side of the boundary, everybody I'd been hanging out with and playing ball with since kindergarten went to a different junior high, Whitman, and I found myself, at age 12, as isolated as I'd ever been. I didn't have one friend in the school, and the humiliation of not having made the SP continued to haunt me—along with everything else that had been haunting me for as long as I could remember. Then one day in gym class, I fell off a chinning bar and landed on my right shoulder. I don't know if it was a pure accident or if I'd unconsciously let myself go flying as I was attempting an acrobatic flip. It happened fast: I was on the bar and then I was on the floor, dazed and surrounded by people. The gym teacher, Mister Schwartz, not only didn't think I needed medical attention, but decided I should get back up on the bar and show him what had happened. So I did, more or less trying to re-create the flip that went awry.

When I got home that afternoon, I told my mother about the accident. She didn't seem concerned.

It was later that night that I stood against the wall in my room staring at the hammer I held in my left hand, thinking it would be better to pound my shoulder with the flat side of the head rather than the rounded side. I'd begin where my collarbone connected to my upper arm and work my way inward, across the collarbone, to my neck. And so I did, first with a couple of tentative taps, then gradually building up force until I smashed the hammer into my shoulder as hard as I could—once, twice, three times. It was on the third smash that I heard something crack. Then, just to make sure it was properly broken, I pounded it three more times with all my strength. I felt no pain. On the contrary, it felt *good*, as if I'd finally achieved a moment of serenity and found an answer to all the questions I could never quite express.

I couldn't sleep that night; my entire body throbbed with pain, and by the next morning my shoulder had turned purple. My mother took me to the emergency room at Methodist Hospital, where X-rays revealed a broken collarbone, a separated shoulder, a punctured lung, and a broken rib, though I don't recall smashing myself in the ribs. Nobody, not even the doctor, seemed to suspect that my injuries were the result of anything other than a gym accident, and I certainly never breathed a word to anyone about what I'd done to myself.

That was how I got my upper-body cast, as well as six weeks of sympathy from my family and the nonstop attention of my friends and former classmates, who covered the cast with their multicolored autographs and doodles. And as an extra-added bonus, I didn't have to do homework or take tests because I couldn't move my arm to write.

What my teachers didn't know was that I had a typewriter, the Olivetti my parents had gotten for me with their Raleigh coupons, and that I could type on it with my left hand. So there in my room, with the door closed and the Beatles playing low on my phonograph for the thousandth time, I sat before the typewriter, which I'd set up on the bridge table that I normally used to do my homework. I had an idea. I wanted to write something for a new TV show that had begun in September, *The Man from U.N.C.L.E.*, a spy series that I liked almost as much as I liked the Beatles.

I began to tap out, with two fingers and a thumb, a script, the opening sequence forming in my head as clearly as if I were watching it on TV: *Air Force One, the president's plane, sits on a tarmac. The cabin door opens and the president appears in the doorway. He begins to walk down the steps. Shots ring out, and the bullets smash into the president's head. He looks stunned as he collapses and tumbles down the stairs. Cue the theme song...*

But I couldn't figure out where to go from there. I tried writing some dialogue for agents Napoleon Solo and Illya Kuryakin as they discussed how to best hunt down the president's evil THRUSH assassins. But unable to establish the lightly comic tone the show was known for, I abandoned the project. It was too hard.

Not long after, my mother picked up for a song, at the Salvation Army, an old desk, which she installed in my room. Over the next month, she artfully refinished it, using little cans of stain to make it look like an expensive antique. By the time my cast came off, not only had I told the story of falling off the chinning bar so many times that I'd convinced myself that it was really how I'd injured my shoulder and rib (somewhere along the way managing to erase the hammer incident from my memory—guilt and shame would keep it buried for another 50 years), but the transformation of the desk was complete. I now had a permanent place to set up my Olivetti, and I found myself typing on it every day, with two hands, not impossible television projects beyond my capabilities, but rather, for my own amusement, imaginary play-by-play calls like I'd hear Marty Glickman do on the radio for Giant games: *Tittle takes the snap from center... drops back to pass... looking downfield... under pressure... throwing long for Shofner...*

This, I thought, was what I really wanted to do; I wanted to write about football and baseball, too, and get paid for it. I wanted to see my name in print. What I didn't know was that waiting for me three light years in the future were a paisley shirt and a *Sgt. Pepper* album, these talismans from across the universe carrying with them unfathomable information, information that would change everything, information that in late 1964 might as well have been science fiction.

20

Far from *Flapbush*

An Epilogue

The summer I turned 20, I toured Israel and worked on a kibbutz outside Jerusalem with "the Czech girl," as I came to think of her. Her name was Naomi, and I'd met her five months earlier, at a party in Midwood, near Brooklyn College, where she was a freshman. We'd shared a joint and talked all night about *Flapbush*, as if it were the old country, and how strange it was that we'd never run into each other before, even though she'd grown up four blocks from where I used to live, and that sometimes, when she got off the subway, she'd stop by my father's candy store to buy a Peter Paul Mounds or an Almond Joy.

A month later, over dinner in Chinatown, she'd told me another story: Just before the war, her grandmother and her father, whom I'd met earlier that night, had escaped from Czechoslovakia on foot, with the Gestapo in hot pursuit. Along with a few thousand other displaced Jews, they wound up in Flatbush. But they were the only ones in her father's family who'd gotten out, she said. The Nazis had murdered everybody else in Auschwitz. Yet every year her father returned to Prague—"for the mineral baths," he always said, but Naomi, her mother, and her grandmother knew that he was really going back to search for another living family member, another survivor. Whom he never found.

Wondering if she usually waited until the third date to lay on the Holocaust story, I listened to her with undivided attention— not because I wanted to hear it, but because she was an adorable, guitar-strumming hippie and I thought there was a pretty good chance she was going to let me sleep with her sooner or later. And then I felt welling up inside me the kind of sadness I hadn't felt in years, something beyond numbness and the desire to change the channel that seemed to overcome me every time somebody started talking about the fucking Holocaust.

"Good God, I'm so sorry," I said, reaching across the table to give her hand a comforting squeeze.

Now, on a July afternoon, our first day off after a week of weeding the kibbutz's Jewish peanut fields under a blazing Jewish sun and helping to inoculate its Jewish chickens with Jewish antibiotics—for it seemed to me that living on that kibbutz, Jewishness was inescapable—Naomi and I stood outside the walls of the Old City of Jerusalem, near the Jaffa Gate, waiting for a bus along with two men, both Auschwitz survivors, as we could see from the numbers on their forearms.

We couldn't have been standing there for more than a few seconds before one of them pointed to us and said something, in Yiddish, to his friend.

A cloud seemed to pass across Naomi's face, and turning to them, she unleashed a furious barrage of curse-laden Yiddish that stunned the men into absolute, jaw-dropping silence.

Bobby in Naziland

Then, in a calmer tone, she said something else, which I didn't understand at all, that the men responded to with solemn nods and profuse apologies.

I looked on, astonished. Never had I seen Naomi yell at anybody like that, and never had I heard her speak more than a handful of the most common Yiddish words, the ones that everybody knew, like *schlep* and *schlump* and *schnook*. I'd still thought the only people who actually spoke the language were old Jews who didn't want young Jews to understand what they were saying.

"What the hell was that all about?" I asked her as we took our seats on the bus.

"They called us 'dirty hippies,'" she said, still angry. "So, I told them, 'How dare you? We work on a kibbutz'... and I told them what happened to my family."

"Since when do you speak fluent Yiddish?"

She laughed. "Since always. It's the only language my grandmother speaks, so I had to learn it."

As I came to understand during that summer of my Middle Eastern sojourn, Yiddish, the international language of the Holocaust and the second language of the Land of Survivors, was something you were required to carry with you when the Nazis had murdered your family. It was the "dead" language that refused to die—along with the knowledge of what had happened to the six million who once spoke it.

This and more the Czech girl carried with her, quietly for the most part. And it carried us through the Promised Land, from the Golan Heights to the Gulf of Aqaba, where we sat one morning after breakfast, 14 miles from the Saudi Arabian border, on the beach in Eilat, looking out at the Red Sea.

I knew then that I was finally far from *Flapbush*, that I *had* gotten out, and that I intended to stay out, though I'd always carry Flatbush with me—as Naomi carried her Yiddish, as my father carried the war.

Afterword

Personal Nazis

Bobby in Naziland is an attempt to make sense of a confusing past that for most of my life I pretended didn't exist. It's autobiography that doesn't adhere strictly to the constraints of time, a series of interconnected riffs and ruminations about growing up lower middle class and Jewish in the Flatbush section of Brooklyn in the interminable aftermath of World War II... a rant in 20 chapters, an adult consciousness channeling the thoughts and emotions of a child. It's the work of a memoirist, a humorist, a historian, a journalist, and a novelist. It's all in there, intertwined like a strand of DNA.

For the record: I've changed some names to protect people's privacy.

The seeds of *Bobby in Naziland* can be found in the opening pages of my previous book, *Beaver Street*—a description of the scene in my father's candy store in 1961. As I wrote those pages, I knew that I was only scratching the surface, and that whatever was happening in Flatbush in the mid-1950s to the mid-1960s, from the final days of the Brooklyn Dodgers to the arrival of the Beatles, was rich material that demanded further exploration. So I wrote down everything I could remember about that time and place, and when I looked back at the 400 single-spaced pages of notes, fragments, anecdotes, and ideas that had accumulated, what jumped out at me were Nazis—they were everywhere, and in one way or another, it was Nazis and the Holocaust that provided much of the inspiration I needed to write this book.

But not all those Nazis are specters from the distant past. Some of them are very much of the present.

Like, in a sense, Donald J. Trump. I wrote *Bobby in Naziland* when he was still the easily ignored ringmaster of a cheesy reality show, a failed casino owner, and a six-times-bankrupted real estate tycoon whose monstrous erections continue to mar the Manhattan skyline. Trump isn't a card-carrying Nazi; he doesn't wear a brown shirt and swastika armband. But he has given aid and comfort to neo-Nazis, notably in Charlottesville, Virginia, when, after a neo-Nazi killed an anti-fascist protester, running her over with his car, he defended the alt-right demonstrators, saying there were "very fine people on both sides."

The pervasive hatred and bigotry that I describe in this book is the same hatred and bigotry that Trump knows intimately, having grown up in Queens, the borough adjoining Brooklyn, in the 1940s and 50s. I'm thinking specifically of the scene in *Bobby in Naziland* where I'm driving around Brooklyn with my father and uncle, and they're telling me things like, "You get two points for every nigger you run down."

This was common behavior at the time, so it would be surprising if Trump were *not* exposed to that kind of bigotry by his father. Fred Trump was a real estate developer who refused to rent apartments to people of color—a policy that, in 1973, brought Donald, then the 26-year-old president of his father's company, his first dose of national media attention. The Justice Department's civil rights division sued Trump Management for racial discrimination. (They settled out of court.)

Bobby in Naziland

Seven years later, just in case anyone doubted the depth of Trump's racism, he took out full-page ads in the local New York newspapers calling for the execution of five young black and Latino men—the "Central Park Five"—convicted of raping and beating a jogger, but later exonerated.

It's this kind of hatred and bigotry, which Trump understood often lurks just below the surface, that he was able to inflame and exploit to become president of the United States.

It was a few years before Trump's ascent to high office, on November 7, 2013, as I was working on an early draft of *Bobby in Naziland*, that an article titled "Swastikas, Slurs, and Torment in Town's School" appeared on the front page of *The New York Times*. It described a series of incidents that I'd been hearing about for years: Jewish high-school students in Pine Bush, a rural community 75 miles north of New York City, had been repeatedly subjected to anti-Semitic behavior, sometimes violent. They were punched and pelted with coins; scores of swastikas were scrawled on the walls of the school; and in one case, a girl's classmate restrained her as another student drew a swastika on her face. Some of the taunts the kids spouted seemed to be relics from the 1940s: "How do you get a Jewish girl's number? You lift up her sleeve."

My brother, referred to in the *Times* as "Jerrold R," is one of the people at the center of this story. His two sons were among the targets of the anti-Semitism, and he and his wife, along with two other families, sued the school district for turning a blind eye to this behavior despite their repeated complaints. New York State and the U.S. Justice Department launched multiple investigations, and in 2015, just before the case went to trial, the school district settled, agreeing to pay the students $4.48 million.

The incident reminded me of my own run-in with anti-Semitism, which had begun about 10 years earlier. That was when I became aware of a Holocaust-denying conspiracy theorist—pseudonymous, naturally—who had read my John Lennon biography, *Nowhere Man*, and had started posting on the Internet his paranoid theories about the book. He accused me of being a Zionist-funded CIA spymaster who'd given the order to kill Lennon, and went on to assert that in order to disgrace Lennon's memory (as well as the entire antiwar movement), the CIA had given me even more money—to write *Nowhere Man*.

Why would the CIA do this? Near as I can tell, the theorist believed that I—along with another Jew, Edward Teller, the "Father of the H-bomb," and Ronald Reagan—felt that Lennon had to die and be completely discredited so America could go forward with its "Star Wars" missile-defense initiative.

Did he have any evidence tying me to the conspiracy? Of course he did! I'd once written speeches for the secretary of the air force—it was an open-and-shut case.

That there are people like this lurking on the Internet should come as no surprise to anybody. That other people who call themselves "journalists" echo such theories in cyberspace and, on occasion, have published them in books, and in at least one legitimate newspaper, is alarming.

I briefly considered dedicating *Bobby in Naziland* as follows: "For _____, my Personal Nazi, who reminded me I was a Jew and taught me anew the meaning of anti-Semitism."

While writing this book, I was also working on a series of satirical videos with Paul Slimak, an actor who has portrayed Nazis both on stage and on such TV shows as *Late Night with Conan O'Brien*. These videos were a vehicle for Slimak's own comedic creation Erich von Pauli, a deranged fugitive from the

Bobby in Naziland

Third Reich who's not yet gotten word that World War II is over.

It was probably inevitable that in the course of our writing these scripts, von Pauli would become a fictional representation of my real Personal Nazi's unbridled id (and the communal id of a certain segment of the Pine Bush student body), and that the dark humor I attempted to infuse into the videos would flow back into *Bobby in Naziland*, commingling with the hard facts of real Nazi atrocities—the very atrocities that my real Personal Nazi, who Slimak didn't even know existed, insists never occurred.

In 1945, during the final days of World War II, as a member of General Patton's 94th Infantry Division, my father, Irwin Rosen, witnessed some of those horrors firsthand when his division liberated a slave labor camp in Germany. He saw the corpses piled high in pyramidal heaps; he saw the starving survivors barely clinging to life; and soon afterwards, he returned to Brooklyn haunted by entire battalions of Personal Nazis. He also brought home with him the souvenirs—the bayonets, medals, swastikas, photos, and stories—that made such an indelible impression upon me so many years ago. He may as well have been whispering in my ear as I was writing *Bobby in Naziland*—sometimes reminding me of long-forgotten tales that should never be forgotten, and other times telling me to forget the unforgettable, which I couldn't do, not in this book anyway.

The End

© Mary Lyn Maiscott

ROBERT ROSEN is the author of the international bestseller *Nowhere Man: The Final Days of John Lennon* and the investigative memoir *Beaver Street: A History of Modern Pornography*. His work has appeared in such publications as *Mother Jones*, *The Soho Weekly News*, *The Independent*, *Uncut*, and *Proceso*. He lives in New York City.

ROBERTROSENNYC.COM

ROBERTROSEN27

RROSEN2727

Acknowledgments

Bobby in Naziland could not have been written, nor could I have had a viable writing career, without an extensive network of people who, for decades, right down to these acknowledgments, have provided critical feedback, legal advice, employment, and emotional, spiritual, and financial support. I give heartfelt thanks to my family, especially my mother, Eleanor Rosen, my late father, Irwin Rosen, and my brother and attorney, Jerrold Rosen, who lived and then transcended what I describe in these pages.

Much credit also goes to my wife and editor, Mary Lyn Maiscott, the Mistress of Syntax, who made this a better book.

Thomas E. Kennedy, Michael Lee Nirenberg, B. A. Nilsson, Doug Garr, David Comfort, Whitney Strub, J. C. Malone, Darius H. James, and A. D. Hitchen were all kind enough to read and critique the manuscript when it was a work in progress.

My friends in New York and around the world, including Joyce Snyder, Sonja Wagner, Dee Burton, Deametrice Eyster, Roberto Ponce, René Portas, Beatriz Norma Iacoviello, Paolo Palmieri, Chris Reeves, and the late Robert Attanasio, as well as my colleagues, past and present, at *Vanity Fair*, have been an inspiration, probably more than they realize.

And special thanks to my editor at Headpress, David Kerekes, who, for almost 30 years, has tended to the flame of independent publishing and who made this book possible.

A HEADPRESS BOOK
First published by Headpress in 2019
headoffice@headpress.com

BOBBY IN NAZILAND
A Tale of Flatbush

Text copyright © ROBERT ROSEN 2017
This volume copyright © HEADPRESS 2019
Cover photo copyright © ROBERT ROSEN
Cover design : MARK CRITCHELL : mark.critchell@googlemail.com
Book layout & design : GANYMEDE FOLEY

10 9 8 7 6 5 4 3 2 1

A CIP catalogue record for this book is
available from the British Library

ISBN   978-1-909394-68-1 (paperback)
ISBN   978-1-909394-69-8 (ebook)
NO-ISBN (hardback)

HEADPRESS. POP AND UNPOP CULTURE.

Exclusive NO-ISBN special edition hardbacks and other
items of interest are available at HEADPRESS.COM